Beginning
the Assistant
Principalship

Beginning the Assistant Principalship

A Practical Guide for New School Administrators

John C. Daresh

CORWIN PRESS
A Sage Publications Company
Thousand Oaks, California

For information:

Corwin Press
A Sage Publications Company
2455 Teller Road
Thousand Oaks, California 91320
www.corwinpress.com

Sage Publications Ltd.
1 Oliver's Yard
55 City Road
London EC1Y 1SP
United Kingdom

Sage Publications India Pvt. Ltd.
B-42, Panchsheel Enclave
Post Box 4109
New Delhi 110 017 India

Printed in the United States of America

Library of Congress Cataloging-in-Publication Data

Daresh, John C.
Beginning the assistant principalship : a practical guide for new school administrators / by John C. Daresh.
   p. cm.
Includes index.
ISBN 0-7619-3991-1 (cloth) — ISBN 0-7619-3992-X (pbk.)
   1. Assistant school principals—United States. 2. First year school principals—United States. 3. School management and organization—United States. 4. Educational leadership—United States. I. Title.
LB2831.92.D35 2004
371.2′012—dc22

                                    2004001139

This book is printed on acid-free paper.

04   05   06   07   08   10 9 8 7 6 5 4 3 2 1

Acquisitions Editor:	Robert D. Clouse
Editorial Assistant:	Jingle Vea, Candice Ling
Production Editor:	Julia Parnell
Copy Editor:	Kristin Bergstad
Proofreader:	Kathrine Pollock
Typesetter:	C&M Digitals (P) Ltd.

Contents

Acknowledgments

I would like to acknowledge the specific contributions of several individuals during the development of this book. First, I thank Charles Vass, currently an administrator in the Gadsden, New Mexico, Schools. Charlie prompted much of my thinking related to the unique role and needs of assistant principals several years ago with a simple observation that universities should really focus their attention on the development of skills for assistant principals because that is where so many people get their start in educational administration. From that first comment, a friendship built on mutual respect has grown over the last several years. In addition, I learned a great deal from Charlie as we cofounded and cofacilitated the Assistant Principal Academy for the Socorro (Texas) Independent School District for a number of years.

I have also learned much from the many students at the University of Texas at El Paso who have stepped into assistant principalships and kept me informed of their insights and experiences. Among those who have been most effective in "keeping me honest" have been John, Roskosky, Marc Escareno, Irma Phillips, Melinda Carey, Carlos Amato, Joe Jacobo, Adrian Botello, Carla Gasway, Teri Gandara, Kim Baxter, Robert Abdou, and many others who are having an impact on schools in El Paso and in other locations across the country.

The ongoing modeling of other excellent school leaders I have known is also represented by this book. Among those that I note here are Nick Cobos, Jim Kelch, Debbie Livingston, Becky Quiett, Maria Gutierrez, Mark Rupcich, Armando Aguirre, and others who have so often shown a sincere commitment to working effectively with assistant principals in their schools.

Whenever I take on a new writing project, I realize how dependent I am on the patience and insights of many other colleagues at the university and elsewhere. Rodolfo Rincones, James Satterfield, Ron Capasso, Bruce Barnett, Sandra Hurley, Gary Brooks, Rick Sorenson, Arturo Pacheco, and Susanna Navarro have all been influential in shaping much of my thinking about educational leadership. Of course, no writing project by a faculty member is ever successful without the ongoing support of the dean, in this case, Josie Tinajero.

My friends at Corwin, particularly Robb Clouse and Douglas Rife, have been available whenever I needed to seek advice or explain another missed deadline.

Finally, I continue to express my sincere appreciation to my wife, Stephanie, and my daughter, Bridget, for their support and patience in this and all my work.

Corwin Press gratefully acknowledges the contributions of the following people:

Lucia V. Sebastian
Principal
James River Elementary School
Williamsburg, VA

Elaine L. Wilmore
Author
Associate Professor, Special
Assistant to the Dean of NCATE
College of Education
The University of Texas at
Arlington
Arlington, TX

Kathy Whitmire
Assistant Superintendent for
Instruction
School District of Oconee County
Walhalla, SC

Ed Poole
Associate Professor
College of Education
Aurora University
Aurora, IL

John A. Beineke
Dean
College of Education
Arkansas State University
State University, AR

Jody S. Piro
Assistant Professor
College of Education
Aurora University
Aurora, IL

Anthony J. Dosen
Assistant Professor
College of Education
DePaul University
Chicago, IL

Paulette Tetteris-Woosley
Assistant Principal
Denton Elementary School
Denton, NC

Jennifer Stair
Title I Teacher and Reading
Coordinator
Cedar Spring Elementary
House Springs, MO

About the Author

 **John C. Daresh** is currently Professor of Educational Leadership and Director of the Principal Preparation Program at the University of Texas at El Paso. He has worked in faculty and administrative positions in higher education for more than twenty years at the University of Cincinnati, The Ohio State University, the University of Northern Colorado, and now in Texas. He has served as a consultant and speaker for school districts, universities, and state departments of education across the United States, Europe, Africa, and Asia. He is an active member and contributor to projects of the National Association of Elementary School Principals and the National Association of Secondary School Principals. He began his career by working in private and public schools in Dubuque, Iowa, and in the Chicago Public Schools. He received his master's degree at DePaul University and doctorate from the University of Wisconsin–Madison.

Among recent books Daresh has completed for Corwin Press are *Leaders Helping Leaders, What It Means to Be a Principal, Teachers Mentoring Teachers,* and *The Beginning Principalship: A Practical Guide for School Leaders.*

To Stephanie and Bridget.
And assistant principals everywhere.

Neither Fish nor Fowl

Diane Lopez and Naomi Garza have been best friends for many years. They worked across the hall from each other as English teachers at Mesa High School, and the two decided to begin graduate studies in educational administration at State University and pursue certification as school principals. Although both were recognized in their district as outstanding teachers, they wanted to do more and become the leaders of schools in the future.

Diane and Naomi took all their classes together. They worked on projects, prepared for exams, and completed their preservice internships at the same school. They became known by State University faculty and other graduate students as the "Mesa Twins" because they were always together. But after completing their studies and passing the state principal certification exam, the two began to apply for different administrative positions in their own school district and other nearby systems.

Naomi was the first to land a job as an assistant principal. She was extremely pleased to become an assistant to Mark Stevens, another former teacher at Mesa and now the principal at Quincy Middle School, an old building serving a middle-class community in the Greenwich Community School District. Mark had taught in the same department as Naomi and Diane for several years, and Naomi felt very comfortable with having a strong potential mentor in her first assignment.

About two weeks later, Diane was asked to take the assistant principalship at a new middle school in her own district, the Wooded Mountain Community School District. The school was set to open the next school year with Diane and Mary Jane Allen as the administrative team. Mary Jane was a newcomer to the district. She had served as a principal of two secondary schools in a district in another state. She had a great deal of prior successful administrative experience, so Diane was looking forward to having the chance to learn from a veteran.

Both Diane and Naomi were happy about their new positions and both looked forward to these positions serving as stepping-stones to their future goals of eventually becoming principals together in the same school district. They often joked about reuniting the Mesa Twins as leaders. For now, however, the "Twins" would be separated for a while so they could learn about becoming effective administrators. Fortunately, both seemed to have landed on their feet by having the opportunity to work in good schools with excellent, well-respected educational leaders. Naomi and Diane promised each other that they would get together at least once a week during the time they served as assistants at their respective schools. They wanted these jobs to serve as learning experiences for their futures, and being able to share war stories regularly would be important ways to gain greater insights into the principalship.

Best intentions, of course, often go awry. From her first day on the job, Naomi realized that she was not going to have any free moments for quite some time. Mark Stevens immediately began to give her one assignment after another. First, he assigned her to do the textbook distribution and inventory for the year. The last assistant principal left in April, so she wasn't around to complete the end-of-year return of books, and the book room was a mess. It was also explained that, because Mark did not have a strong background in special education, the new assistant principal would be expected to devote her time to that program area this next year. He concluded his first meeting with Naomi by informing her that he would be out of town at the state principals' meeting for the next three days, so she would be in charge during his absence. While she was mentally recording the "laundry list" of duties she was just handed, Naomi recognized that this new job was going to keep her busy day and night for quite some time.

Diane was also experiencing a number of reservations about her job. She thought that it was going to be fairly simple since she was going to be opening a school with a principal who did not really know much about the district. She anticipated that she would be learning along with her boss. Diane probably knew more teachers in the school than the principal. At least four people had worked with her at Mesa over the years, and another handful of people were former teachers from Diane's old district. She was hoping that knowing a number of the teachers would make her transition to the assistant principalship a lot easier. But the principal had her assigned to do so many things during the first few weeks that she spent hardly any time with her old friends. And as the school year began, the teachers were also busy, and the assistant principal's chores just continued to grow.

What was supposed to be a regular occurrence for the two friends—getting together once a week—became a special event in late September when Naomi and Diane finally found one night when they could have dinner. Naomi and Diane each began their meal by joking about how tired the other looked. After a few minutes, they settled into a conversation that reflected why they were so fatigued in their new jobs.

"It's a lot different from what I expected," started Diane. "There are ten times more things to do than I thought there would be. And what's getting me down is the way things are going with some of the teachers. I've known many folks for years, but no one comes around to see how I'm doing, or if I need any help. And I know that I'm definitely not one of the administrators yet, but some teachers still appear to avoid me because they view me as 'one of them.'"

"Yeah, I know that feeling," said Naomi. "I was sure that Mark was going to take a little bit of pity on me as a rookie. But the job is really demanding, and I feel like I can't catch my breath. It's really a lot of work, and even with an old friend like Mark as my boss, the job keeps me busy all the time. I really hope that he still respects me as his colleague."

The next hour was spent sharing similar observations about their new jobs, and also some of the jobs that they were expected to do. The Mesa Twins went their separate ways without even having dessert. After all, both had early duties tomorrow and no doubt stacks of student discipline referrals on their desks.

People pursue the position of assistant principal for many reasons. For some, it represents an opportunity to earn a salary that is higher than one makes as a classroom teacher (in most cases). In other cases, people see the role of assistant as a necessary first step toward eventually becoming a school principal. After becoming assistant principals, some people realize that this job is sufficiently rewarding or challenging, and they no longer seek a principalship. But regardless of what the short-term or long-term goals of any single aspiring assistant principal may be, most people who take on this job make the assumption that it is an important leadership role in schools. A person needs to be capable, dedicated, and responsible to become an administrator, at any level. As is the case for our two beginning assistants in the opening scenario, people discover quickly that the assistant principalship is very demanding in terms of time, energy, and personal dedication. They also begin to find out that it can be a frustrating role.

Why is it frustrating? Beyond the fact that the job requires a great commitment of time and energy, there is an even more pronounced aspect of the job that catches many people by surprise. Being an assistant principal can often be summed up by the phrase "neither fish nor fowl." When you take on an assistant principalship, you enter a kind of "gray world." You are no longer a classroom teacher, although you may feel as if that is still where you work. After all, you just spent at least (in most school districts and states) three years as a teacher before you qualified for an administrative certificate or license. The challenging aspect of this is that, even though you might still identify as being a teacher, you are not. Your former colleagues in the classroom will tell you very quickly that you are no longer part of their group. You will often feel the separation and isolation from the classroom very quickly. Conversations between teachers will stop abruptly when you approach, informal conversations with people in the hall or out in the parking lot will begin to become rare, and your old friends will not be stopping by your office regularly. Friday afternoons at the local watering hole will not be the same—after all, "the administration" is often a topic during "TGIF" sessions.

Another perspective is that you are *only an assistant principal.* That means that, in the minds of many veteran administrators in your district, you are not yet "one of them." Many principals and other district administrators remember that they, too, were once assistants on individual campuses. That's how they got their start in administration. You will hear many fond (or not so fond) recollections of the days "when I was an assistant principal," as if it were like a period of hazing that people have to endure if they eventually want to land a "real job." For the most part, assistant principals will work with principals and other administrators who are sympathetic to their colleagues and their roles. On the other hand, you may encounter a principal who truly believes that it is best to treat assistant principals in the ways that new army recruits are treated during boot camp. There is still a sense among many administrators that they "learned it the hard way—on their own." They use that as their justification for making things less than wonderful learning experiences for assistants.

As a beginning assistant principal, you have probably just completed a preservice certification program at a local university where the curriculum included a great deal of information concerning "leadership" as opposed to "management." You have heard descriptions of how effective school leaders are critical ingredients of effective schools. You have also heard many stories about the central role that instructional leadership plays by building administrators and that this is vital to ensure increases in student learning and achievement. If school administrators spend less time with management issues and more time with curriculum development and monitoring the teaching and learning activities of their schools, they will be more effective.

So what are you doing as an administrator? Disciplining students, sitting in on what often seem to be endless court hearings, working with custodial staff, keeping track of textbooks, and handling parking lot (or bus) duty before and after school. There is not much time left for leading the school in such weighty matters as curricular reform, staff development, or vision setting. If your personal goal is to become a principal some day, none of these duties may seem to have much relevance. Remember, however, that serving as an assistant principal of a school can be understood in broader terms, as seen through a comparison with other professional roles. There are *assistant* coaches of World Champion basketball teams and Super Bowl–winning football teams, and assistant managers of Fortune 500 corporations. All of these are critical contributors to their organization's success. They are all similar to assistant principals because they are not necessarily classified as "chief executives." Nevertheless, they add much to overall success.

From the perspective of your former colleagues in the classroom, you seem to spend most of your day doing things that have little to do with supporting teachers. In fact, you are absent from classrooms except for those moments when you must do some required teacher observations.

In short, you are neither the fish in charge of anything nor part of the flock of fowl. That is one of the main reasons why I believe that your service as an assistant principal might be one of the more difficult educational jobs that a person can do. Teachers know what they are supposed to do every day—they teach—and principals are hired to lead, or at least "run the school." Counselors counsel. Assistant principals, on the other hand, do a lot of things that do not appear on the list of normal, routine activities of any school.

PROBLEM WITH DEFINITION

The frustrations you may feel concerning the lack of precise identification of your duties may be the product of some long-standing lack of clarity about what assistant principals are supposed to do. Assistant administrators in public schools have been identified as important workers in schools for many years. For example, one of the earliest scholars of school administration, Ellwood P. Cubberly (1916), noted that assistants could be quite helpful in doing many of the things that were beyond the scope of duties that were most important for lead administrators of schools. One example of a "nonessential" duty that could be delegated to an assistant is the visitation of teachers in their classrooms.

Kyte (1952) noted the following with regard to the duties and responsibilities that should be assigned by a principal:

> The assistant principal should be assigned to specific responsibilities and duties. He may have some teaching assignment, but the remainder of his school time he should spend on the work of the principalship. In many schedules, his teaching is limited to planned substitution in all classes. Thus, he obtains teaching experience on all grade levels and in various phases. This practical exposure contributes to his insights into teachers' problems and needs and to his understanding of all children. (p. 394)

In this instance, the assistant principal is viewed as a candidate for future principal responsibilities by gaining insights into curriculum and instructional practices. Kyte also notes, however, that the assistant principal has many other responsibilities in the course of each day, as noted in the following schedule for a "typical Monday":

8:00–8:30 Inspect the school plant

8:30–9:00 Confer with parents, children, and teachers; assign new pupils to classes; handle minor discipline cases; supervise junior traffic squads; supervise playgrounds, corridors, and boys' lavatories.

9:00–10:30 Teach fourth grade

10:30–10:45 Recess duty

10:45–11:15 Visit Kindergarten and primary grades, observing activities and reading; study individual cases assigned by principal either on teacher's request or for other reasons; give needed demonstration lessons

11:15–12:00 Teach fourth grade

12:00–12:20 Supervise lunchroom and junior traffic squads; lunch

12:20–1:00 Confer with parents, children, and teachers; supervise junior traffic squads; supervise playground, corridors, and boys' lavatories

1:00–2:00 Supervise office staff; direct assemblies

2:00–3:10 Spend time in supervisory activities

3:10–4:10 Participate in building and group meetings

After presenting this ideal work schedule for an assistant principal, Kyte then notes an actual record of a 1950s assistant principal's duties for one day:

8:00–8:25 Conferred with Miss S. about the reading observed in her class yesterday; I am to help her regroup her children

8:25–8:35 Conferred with new pupil and his mother; assigned him to third grade; introduced them to Mrs. G.

8:35–8:40 Advised Mrs. G. to check on child to see if he belongs a half grade higher

8:40–9:00 Supervised the Second Avenue Traffic squad, with special attention to the new lieutenant's work

9:00–10:30 Taught class

10:30–10:45 Conferred with new lieutenant regarding timing the use of his whistle and waiting until all children reach the sidewalk; checked boys' lavatory

10:45–11:15 Observed second grade class; commended Miss L. on extent of pupil participation with interest

11:15–12:00 Taught class

12:00–12:40 Lunch period

12:40–1:00 Observed on the school grounds, Miss B. and Miss W. being in charge; requested Miss B. to test the new boy tomorrow, discussing the case with her

1:00–1:15 Conferred with parent regarding her son's frequent tardiness

1:15–2:00 Discussed with Miss W. and her class the care and use of cutting tools, demonstrating usage

2:00–2:05 Observed traffic in the upper hall; noticed congestion still occurring near west stairway

2:05–3:10 Discussion with school secretary on method of scoring tests and sample checking the scored results; dictated short statement on diagnostic use of the results; dictated note to Mrs. S. about upper hall congestion; checked classification report

3:10–3:20 Reported to Miss W. the agreement reached with parent about the tardy pupil

3:20–3:50 Conferred with Mrs. R. regarding the science lesson observed yesterday; she is to encourage more diversified interests, providing for more planned excursions to the park

3:50–4:20 Conferred with Mr. S. about Miss M.'s problems in handcrafts; made a memorandum of suggestions to be included in my conference with her

As you review these lists of planned and actual duties of the assistant principal of 50 years ago, you are no doubt struck by a number of issues. First, note the fact that assistant principals are described in masculine terms. On the other hand, with one exception, teachers appear to be women. When "Mr. M. is brought into the discussion," it is to tell him about a (woman) teacher's problems. Second, there is little discussion of the work of the assistant in responding to discipline situations. Not once in these lists is there a description of an unruly student being sent to the office by a teacher.

Third, there is no reference to the assistant being involved with special education matters, no doubt because schools simply did not deal with special education issues a half century ago. Fourth, the assistant principal was a teacher, at least for a short period of time each day. And above all, the supervision and oversight of "traffic squads" was a major concern for the assistant principal. Also, note that the work day seemed to end at a reasonable hour so that the principal could probably get home in time for a family dinner, helping his children with homework, conversing with his wife, reading the newspaper, and many other regular evening activities at home.

Although it may be somewhat amusing to see how the old-time assistant principal enjoyed a different set of daily activities, it is also important to note that the assistant of the past was busy all day long and engaged in a wide variety of activities.

In your experience as an assistant principal, take an "average" day and record the events that you carry out during the day.

_____

_____

_____

_____

In addition to the differences already noted, what are some more things that you do now that were not part of the world of a 1950s assistant principal?

_____

_____

_____

_____

No doubt you indicated that you do a lot more student disciplinary work now, more special education conferencing, and perhaps more in-class observations of teaching. You may also be responsible for the management of certain aspects of the physical plant, but you probably do not have the inclination to dictate memos to teachers about their control of students near one stairway or another. In short, you live a much more reactive work life than your predecessors. Rarely are you able to predict what you will be doing each day, or even from one moment to the next. It is largely because of this fact that your role might become stressful and difficult to manage. No two days are alike, and you have to be able to respond to many different issues that are likely to come across your desk. At the same time, you need skills in dealing with your principal, the teachers, students, parents, police, central office administrators, nonteaching staff, media, and people from the community. The list of interactions of the assistant principal of the past is much shorter than your daily work routines.

A few years ago, the National Association of Secondary School Principals carried out a survey of assistant principals across the nation to identify the kinds of duties they faced each day (Pellicer, Anderson, Keefe, Kelly, & McLeary, 1988) from "most frequent" to "least frequent." The following list was generated:

1. Student discipline
2. Evaluation of teachers
3. Student attendance
4. School policies
5. Special arrangements
6. School master schedule
7. Emergency arrangements
8. Instructional methods

9. Building use—school related

10. Orientation programs for new students

11. Administrative representative at community functions

12. Informing public of school achievement

13. Graduation activities

14. Orientation program for new teachers

15. Faculty meetings

16. Substitute teachers

17. Teacher selection

18. Curriculum development

19. Teacher "duty" rosters

20. Assemblies

21. School public relations program

22. Innovations, experiments, and research

23. School daily bulletins

24. Liaison with community youth-serving agencies

25. Clerical services

26. Teacher incentives, motivation

27. School dances

28. Staff inservices

29. School calendars

30. School club programs

In this whole list of many duties assigned to assistant principals, there is no mention of one item that seemed to be so important in the past—checking on boys' lavatories! Having made that observation, no doubt every assistant principal in the United States has made unannounced visits to school rest rooms—boys' *and* girls'.

The list developed through research by the National Association of Secondary School Principals contains several items (e.g., "Graduation activities") that may not concern you if you work in a middle school or elementary school. But there are many items on the list that are probably part of your regular routine. The one thing that is remarkable in the research from less than twenty years ago is that no mention is made of one of the responsibilities that has become a central part of the world of so many modern assistants—working with special education issues. No doubt the majority of assistant principals today serve as liaison administrators in conferences designed to develop Individual Education Plans for special needs students.

In the space below, list the top ten (or even top eleven) activities that you now carry out on a regular basis. Compare this list with the preceding NASSP research.

_____

_____

_____

_____

_____

THE INVISIBILITY FACTOR

The role of assistant principal is filled with many contradictions. For example, in many schools, when a parent or community member wants to "talk to an administrator," that administrator will often be an assistant principal. In many cases, this is done not to shield the principal from visitors but to serve as a kind of "steering mechanism" that will help the visitor connect with the most appropriate staff member. In that respect, the assistant is a visible person representing the official interests of the school. Yet assistant principals at many schools are often virtually invisible to the public. They do their work in their offices, or as members of committees, or with individual students. They rarely get the recognition commensurate with the work that they do for the school. It is interesting to note that, for example, statewide directories of schools include the names of principals but rarely the names of assistants.

This discrepancy between the assigned duties of assistant principals and their public importance is another example of the mixed messages that are often given regarding this educational role. Schools are in critical need of assistant principals, principals fight hard to retain their lieutenants when there is talk of cutbacks during budget crises, and a resource sought in cases where there are enrollment increases is inevitably another assistant principal. By contrast, assistant principals tend to do their work backstage most of the time. The "neither fish nor fowl" description fits.

What are some of the ways in which you have felt as if you were an "invisible resource" in your school?

_____

_____

_____

_____

SO WHY DO THE JOB?

With all the frustrations and contradictions concerning the role of the assistant principal, it may seem strange that you—or anyone else—would ever want to have the job. Despite the fact that there currently exists a national shortage of people interested in serving as school administrators, we are fortunate that many still want to take on the challenges of a job as complex and often ill defined as the assistant principalship. But the question remains, "Why?"

There are many possible answers to this question. The most critical one, however, is the one that you provide in your own case. Why did you become an assistant principal? (Or, why are you seeking a job as an assistant principal?)

_____

_____

_____

_____

For many, the response provided may be quite similar to yours. You may have stated that you are (or will be) an assistant principal because it is the path that you believe must be followed on your way to other administrative roles in education. In many cases, candidates for principalships will not be considered unless they have three or more years of experience as an assistant. In this regard, service as an assistant principal is seen as a means to a goal, not an end goal in itself. "You have to put in your time" may be the motto of many who step into the assistant job.

Related to this "dues-paying" motivation is the reason offered by many other assistant principals. They realize that being a principal is a difficult and demanding job for which they could hardly be well prepared through any university preservice training program. As a result, there are those who view the assistant principalship as a kind of intense, long-term internship where it is possible to learn much about the practice and reality of the principalship. You may also have stated that your goal is to serve students and your school as a career assistant principal; you do not wish to move up to become a principal.

You may also believe that taking on the assistant principalship is a way to serve the broad interests of a whole school, not just an individual classroom. Accepting an assistant leadership role can allow a serious commitment to service. Chief executives are not the only ones who can contribute to students and teachers.

No doubt many other reasons can be identified to explain why you and others have decided to take on the ambiguous and challenging job of a school assistant principal.

PLAN FOR THE BOOK

In the remaining chapters of this book, the assumption will be made that, regardless of why you became (or will become) an assistant principal, you will hold that position for the foreseeable future. I also believe that you want to do an excellent job as a school leader. This first chapter has pointed out some of the difficulties that assistant principals have always faced as part of their jobs. Assistants are often caught in the crossfire of competing expectations and ideal role definitions held by administrators on one hand and teachers on the other. Or, they are viewed as outsiders by both of these groups.

Assistants have a lot of different duties and responsibilities on the job, from serving the needs of special education students to evaluating teachers to disciplining students to monitoring bathrooms. And to top all of this off, not many people seem to recognize or appreciate what assistant principals do each day.

The remaining chapters of this book consider a wide variety of topics that are introduced as a way to help you succeed in your current job, whether your intentions are to use your experience as an assistant to qualify for a principalship, use your current job as a kind of internship, or if you have decided to make this job your goal as an administrator. We begin with a consideration of how to analyze your personal values and your strengths and limitations both as a leader and as a manager of a school. Then, we look at a number of specific suggestions designed to help you succeed each day as an assistant principal.

REFERENCES

Cubberly, Ellwood P. (1916). *Public school administration*. New York: Macmillan.
Kyte, George C. (1952). *The principal at work* (Rev. ed). Boston: Ginn and Company.
Pellicer, Leonard O., Anderson, Lorin W., Keefe, James W., Kelly, Edgar A., & McLeary, Lloyd E. (1988). *High school leaders and their schools: Vol. 1. A national profile*. Reston, VA: National Association of Secondary School Principals.

SUGGESTED ADDITIONAL READING

Marshall, Catherine. (1992). *The assistant principal: Leadership choices and challenges*. Newbury Park, CA: Corwin Press.
Weller, L. David, & Weller, Sylvia J. (2002). *The assistant principal: Essentials for effective school leadership*. Thousand Oaks, CA: Corwin Press.

2

It Begins With Values

Beginning school administrators experience difficulties during their first years on the job for many reasons. In some cases they do not "take care of business." For example, they might ignore the importance of completing assigned administrative tasks in a timely fashion, or they might violate local policies or even state laws. Another reason for people getting into trouble is that they do not seem to have the kind of people skills needed to communicate effectively with parents, students, staff, teachers, and other administrators. In this chapter, however, the focus is on yet another problem area for leaders. Often, administrators do not recognize the importance of being able to come to grips with personal values and priorities as they carry out their duties. It is critical to be comfortable with your personal values and beliefs. More than anything else you may do as an assistant principal, this is the foundation you will need as you proceed through the remainder of your career. Simply stated, if you don't know who you are and what you believe, it will be virtually impossible to have the ability to influence others so that you can lead them in achieving the goals and vision of their organization.

This chapter suggests a strategy that might be used to identify important personal and professional values as a critical first step toward achieving success as an educational administrator.

CASE STUDY: BECAUSE I BELIEVE IT'S THE RIGHT THING TO DO

Mario Ramirez had been an assistant principal at Capistrano Elementary School in Frontera City for nearly one full year. He really liked the school and the community it served. It reminded him so much of the little town on the U.S.-Mexican border where he grew up. Many of the issues and problems that had faced his parents were now part of his own everyday experience in the area surrounding Capistrano.

A few days ago, Mrs. Chavez, the attendance clerk for the school, came to Mario with a concern regarding one of the new students who came to Mr. Carson's third-grade class. She explained that she was quite sure that the little boy was not really living at the address that his mother gave when she brought him to the school to register last Wednesday. She knew the apartment building whose address was given, and she also knew the manager. There was a family with the name given for the new third grader living at that location, but according to the manager, the mother and boy did not seem to meet the description of the people living in the apartment. Mrs. Chavez admitted that the mother and her son were very polite and friendly people, and so far Mr. Carson had nothing but praise for the boy's behavior in his class. Still, the attendance clerk was well known (and praised) for her strict enforcement of district policy regarding the admission of students from outside the district. She came to Mr. Ramirez immediately when she started to discover evidence of the residence questions because Mario had been assigned the duty of overseeing attendance issues by Dana Earheart, the principal.

"Mr. Ramirez, I sincerely doubt that our new student qualifies as a resident of our attendance area, and there is no record of his mother seeking a district waiver. In my experience here, that often means that the child is actually a resident of Mexico, and we need to start the process of requesting the family to declare 'Out of District' status so that we can collect tuition." Not only did the attendance clerk want to enforce a policy, but she also had a strong sense of trying to ensure that all students in the district were enrolled and they "paid their fare share"—either because of their payment of taxes or as tuition-paying students.

Mario listened patiently to the clerk's explanation, but about halfway through the conversation, he decided that this was going to be a policy that he was simply going to ignore. The little boy was no trouble; in fact, Mario had met him yesterday and was really impressed that he was bright, serious, and an excellent student. He was also quite poor. Mario was simply not going to try to make life even more difficult for this child. After all, the story could have been written about young Mario twenty-five years ago, when he was an "illegal" student as well. This was one place where Mario would have to draw a line between his beliefs and those who worried about attendance policies. In his mind, it was the right thing to do.

School administrators make hundreds of decisions every day. Each is made through certain lenses that individuals bring to the job, and the sources of those lenses vary. Some come from written school board policy manuals. For example, an assistant principal scans the first few referral slips found on her desk in the morning, all written by different teachers describing the misbehavior of different students in their classes yesterday afternoon. Basically, the offenses are the same, but committed by different students known to the assistant. As she reviews the names on the forms, she decides to give one student detention, another one three days of in-school suspension, and for the third student, the assistant principal simply decides to go talk to the teacher and request that the student be allowed to apologize and return to class this morning. Assistant principals and other administrators are called upon to make judgments on similar matters and hand down decisions that are not easily defined and are not readily made according to existing policy in a school or district.

Consider, for example, decisions such as the one Mario made at Capistrano Elementary School. He had to decide what to do with the information he was provided about the residency status of one his students. What was the deciding factor? Mario's personal and professional values had a lot to do with his ultimate choice (and also the probable consequences resulting from his decision). Mr. Ramirez valued providing some students an opportunity to receive a decent education in the United States. That was more important than worrying about enforcing immigration policies or school district residency requirements.

Most decisions made by school administrators are matters of personal choice. In many cases, the reasons that assistant principals use in making their decisions are not clear to the outside observer. Larry Powell is given a three-day suspension, but Art Smith is simply reprimanded for the same offense and sent back to the classroom. Teachers often complain because they see what appear to be inconsistencies in the visible behavior and actions of the assistant principal. Yet, assistant principals often do not seem concerned about what others believe are differential patterns in their behavior. However, experienced administrators have learned—often the hard way—that differences in perceptions, whether they are right or wrong, represent real beliefs and views by others. As a consequence, these perceptions must be understood, appreciated, and ultimately addressed.

Full awareness of one's duties and responsibilities in a job comes about largely as a result of a reflective process in which one constantly matches the requirements of the job with a personal value system. The more a person is content with a choice of career consistent with the most important attitudes, values, and beliefs that drive the person, the happier he or she will be—and more effective, productive, and ultimately successful. It is a simple fact that a person who is more invested in a job as a personal commitment will not only be more satisfied but more effective as well.

The strategy suggested here is a periodic review of something called a *personal educational platform*. Thomas Sergiovanni and Robert Starrat (1979) coined this term to describe ongoing personal reflection and review of professional values for educational supervisors. A platform is a philosophical statement that enables a person to put into writing some of the nearest and dearest beliefs about the educational issues that define a major part of the person's work life. It is often said that the major planks of a platform express an individual's nonnegotiable values. In many ways, they represent the person's core values—the kinds of things that, if violated by the nature of one's job or other factors, would cause the person to quit the job. A personal educational platform has the power on paper to serve as the bottom line for an individual educator, or, as one colleague stated, "The kind of issue that a person might risk even if would mean getting fired."

Finally, a platform statement has the potential either (a) to guide a person away from a professional role that is inconsistent with personal values, or simply (b) to enable a person to know when a particular placement in a job is not what was envisioned in the first place. For example, a platform can help a person to recognize whether selecting the assistant principalship in a specific community was the best move. In either case, if the personal values that are expressed in a platform are not attainable in a job in a particular location, it may be reasonable to move on.

BUILDING A PLATFORM

The pages that follow will lead you through the development of an educational platform. Many different approaches might be followed in carrying out this exercise. You are invited to modify anything offered here so that it is more consistent with your own needs, interests, and, of course, personal values.

You will be asked several questions that have to do with central issues faced by educators, in most cases regardless of whether they work in classrooms or administrative offices. After each question, space is provided for you to write your response. Simply filling in the blanks does not necessarily mean that you have prepared an educational platform. However, your answers below might serve as an important foundation for a more cohesive statement that you will craft at some point in the future.

1. **What is my view of the purpose of schooling?**
People have struggled with this issue for almost as long as there have been formal organizations called schools. Is it your view that students attend these formal organizations to acquire vocational skills? For moral development? To develop basic skills? To learn good citizenship and other core values? Perhaps other purposes guide your vision, as noted below:

_____

_____

_____

_____

2. **What are the key ingredients of an "adequate" education for all students?**
There has been a lot of talk about how to get schools "back to basics." Although this phrase has become a kind of slogan for a particular

conservative point of view regarding schooling, each educator must have some sense of what the basic elements of good schooling might include.

_____

_____

_____

_____

3. What is the appropriate role for students?

Perhaps an even more important issue to be considered here concerns one's personal view of who students are. It is widely assumed that educators all have a core value that speaks to the centrality of the needs of pupils as the driving force in schools. Although this may sound appealing and "right," is it truly your vision and value? _____

_____

_____

_____

_____

4. What is the appropriate role for teachers?

Again, the question might revolve around your personal definition of who teachers are in the first place. Some people view teachers as true professionals who have the best interests of students in mind as they proceed with their duties. Others view teachers as district employees who can be replaced with others who have the same certification and academic degrees. Others might hold views that are between these two opposite perspectives. Are these views consistent with your perspective, or do you have other notions of who teachers are and what they should be doing in schools?

_____

_____

_____

_____

5. What is the appropriate role for parents and other community members?

Most schools greet visitors with a sign or decal on the front door with a statement such as, "Welcome! This is your school." But do you mean that? Are parents truly partners in the educational program or are they intruders? What about the great majority of community members out there who pay taxes but who do not have children enrolled in your (or any other) school? What are your views about the appropriate relationship with private businesses in your local community? _____

_____

_____

_____

_____

6. What is my personal definition of "curriculum"?

Modern definitions of effective school administrators note that they are instructional, or curricular, leaders. What does this mean in practice? Part of it must be based on one's ability to have a clear understanding of what the curriculum is and what it should be in a particular school setting. For example, how inclusive should a school's curriculum be? _____

_____

_____

_____

_____

7. What do I want this school to become?

What is your personal vision for the school? What kinds of hopes and dreams for a more effective school drive your work? What are your ideals? _____

_____

_____

_____

_____

8. How will I know if students have learned?

The ultimate goal of any school must be to ensure that learning has taken place among students. But what are the indicators, at least in your mind, of whether or not this has really taken place? Some say that students' scores on standardized achievement tests are valid indicators, whereas some say learning really occurs only when established outcomes or performances are reached. What is your answer? _____

_____

_____

_____

_____

9. How do I want others to see me?

It is important for a leader to reflect on the kinds of images projected to followers. How do you hope you will be viewed by your teachers, staff, students, parents, and community members? Think about this issue in two ways, as a principal and also as a person. _____

_____

_____

_____

_____

10. What are my nonnegotiable values?

This final question might be the single most important issue to be addressed in your platform. Ultimately, this question asks you to consider the kinds of things that, if violated by the system or by the people with whom you must work, would cause you to throw your keys on the table and seek employment elsewhere. _____

_____

_____

_____

_____

WHAT DO YOU DO WITH THE PLATFORM?

The value in an educational platform is not found by simply writing it out one time, putting it in a file cabinet, and then letting it sit there for the rest of your professional life. Rather, it should be seen as a living document or statement of the parameters that will guide you in making decisions throughout your career. Your platform will change as you move through your professional life. For example, your thinking about the desirability of standardized testing as a way to measure student growth and progress may change drastically from day to day until some point in the future. Your vision of "perfect" teachers may be modified greatly as you move farther away from your days in that same role.

The development of a formal statement of values through the educational platform has many important applications that can be of great assistance to you as you travel through your career as an educational leader. For one thing, developing clarity regarding your nonnegotiable values— even though these might change in the future—can be a genuine help to you as you think about changing jobs, applying for a principalship, moving to other districts, accepting transfers within the school system, and so forth. For example, there are administrators who have decided against higher paying or more prestigious leadership roles because taking these jobs might cause them to compromise more important professional values, such as being able to stay at home with their family, or continuing to work with minority populations.

Second, a clear statement of an educational platform is of value to those with whom you are to work, both those at your individual school site and coworkers across your district. It isn't a good idea to print multiple copies of your platform and send them around to everyone you might meet, however. People who from time to time have made the effort to write their platforms inevitably have a stronger grasp of their own values, so that those around them are also able to see what makes them tick. This not only has the benefit of enabling assistant principals to be open to their staffs, but it is also a powerful way to model communication skills that lead to more effective schooling in general. In the long run, becoming clearer about your personal educational values will assist you in those cases in which you may be seeking other professional positions. For example, an opening for a principalship, particularly one in another school district that may seem more prestigious than your current system, might not be nearly as desirable once you consider some of the possible compromises that might be needed with regard to your personal values and priorities.

Finally, the ultimate value of developing a clear statement of an educational platform may be that it can serve as the foundation for long-term professional development. Too often, educators simply drift through their careers and engage in sporadic and periodic programs of professional development based on learning more about one hot topic or another, or because the central office has made it clear that "all assistant principals must learn about our district's new policy." In many cases, assistant principals simply respond to the platforms of others. It would be far more desirable for assistant principals to engage in systematic career planning that is rooted in their own values and sense of where they are going or what is important to them. For this reason, it is often suggested that people begin their professional development portfolios with a clear statement of their platforms. In that way, other elements of the portfolios are able to flow in a logical sequence from a strong foundation.

YOUR PERSONAL PLAN

In the next few pages, sketch out some of the more critical elements of your personal portfolio and growth plan. You may wish to consult and respond to the questions posed earlier, or you may respond to other critical issues that will provide a greater sense of who you are as a professional educator.

_____

_____

_____

_____

Now that you have written the planks of your platform, the last step in this self-improvement process involves a clear statement of what you plan to do to implement your personal vision of effective practice. Once you have completed this last step, a final valuable activity involves sharing your statement with one or two close friends, your principal, family members, or colleagues with a simple request that they indicate whether or not they recognize in you some of what you have written and whether or not you have written a real or an ideal description. _____

_____

_____

_____

_____

REFERENCE

Sergiovanni, T., & Starrat, R. (1979). _Supervision: Human perspectives._ New York: McGraw-Hill.

SUGGESTED ADDITIONAL READING

Barnett, B. (1991). *The educational platform: A developmental activity for preparing moral school leaders.* Paper presented at the Annual Meeting of the American Educational Research Association, Chicago.

Daresh, J. C. (1982). *Beginning the principalship.* Thousand Oaks, CA: Corwin Press.

Kottkamp, R. (1982). The administrative platform in administrator preparation. *Planning and Changing, 13,* 82–92.

West, S. (1993). *Educational values for school leadership.* London: Kogan Page.

3

A Personal Leadership Checklist

After interviews at five different schools, Adrian Grimaldi got the telephone call he had been awaiting ever since he completed the principal certification program at Greenleaf University. Dora Clements, principal of Hawkins Elementary School, called to ask if he was still interested in serving as her new assistant principal. It was only two days after his interview, and he was caught a bit off guard. After a brief pause in the conversation with Dora, his response was an enthusiastic, "Yes!" This job represented the fulfillment of a major professional goal that Adrian had identified about five years ago, after seven years as a classroom teacher in a school district neighboring the one in which Hawkins Elementary School was located. Adrian had seen the importance of strong leadership in an effective school, and he wanted to contribute to serving as a leader some day. That day had now arrived.

One of the first things Adrian did after signing his contract to start his new job in July was to begin listing some of the things that he wanted to do to become better prepared. He contacted the State Department of Education's Web site to review Hawkins's annual test score reports for the past five years. He had looked at current data while preparing for his interview, but now he wanted to look at trends over several years. Next, he called some friends who had some contact with Hawkins during the past year or two. These included two parents of Hawkins pupils, and two teachers in Adrian's current district who once worked at his future school. Next, he reviewed some of the notes he had taken in some of the classes he considered particularly useful at Greenleaf U. He also called Dr. Herman Hinojosa, his master's degree advisor, for some tips on how he might get ready for his new challenge. After all, Adrian wanted this assistant principalship to be a success.

"It sounds like you've already done a pretty good job getting ready so far, Adrian," was Dr. Hinojosa's first comment. "But one of the things that a lot of beginning administrators neglect to do is to take stock of their strengths and weaknesses as a leader before they start their first jobs. You'll regret it later if you don't start out with a good look at yourself."

Although Adrian doubted that doing a self-inventory on leadership skills would be as important as looking over his school's past test scores, he trusted Dr. Hinojosa's judgment about a lot of things, so he decided to take his advice on this matter.

A few months into his first year at Hawkins, Adrian began to reflect on the value of the professor's suggestion. Throughout the year the assistant principal found challenges that tested his leadership skills. He found that certain issues, particularly those dealing with his personal ability to solve problems, identify trends, share his personal vision and values, communicate, and, above all, work effectively with people were often more important than demonstrating a knowledge of school law or the ability to build a school budget. And he also learned another reality of school administration: Learn how to lead by relying on others to work with you. The important lesson that Adrian learned after his initial review of leadership skills was that he noted where he would likely need some additional guidance from his principal, the teachers, staff, and others.

Adrian realized that he was off to a much better start than if he had simply spent all of his time reviewing last year's achievement scores. As a leader, he was going to look forward, not just look backward.

Adrian Grimaldi is not unusual. Too often, beginning assistant principals invest so much time in finding their first job, getting the school year started, making a good impression on teachers and staff, and keeping their buildings open and well maintained that they ignore the importance of checking out their effectiveness as leaders. There is much to do in order to be an effective school administrator. The key is the person's ability to understand the most critical dimensions of leadership associated with the assistant principalship.

In this chapter, we explore a few leadership frameworks that you may wish to review as a way of assessing your strengths and limitations as a leader. From time to time you may wish to return to this chapter during your first year or two as an assistant to see what progress you are making toward your goal of becoming an effective leader.

LEADERSHIP SKILLS

One of the most popular traditional ways to learn about leadership is through a review of attributes or skills associated with effective leadership performance. There are many types of these lists of specific skills. A walk through the "Management" or "Leadership" sections of any bookstore will reveals dozens if not hundreds of books that provide even more descriptions of leadership characteristics. You may wish to consult any of these references in your search for a helpful framework to guide your own development. A few lists that might be particularly appropriate for an individual who wants to chart personal progress toward becoming an effective school leader are those proposed by the Association for Supervision and Curriculum Development (ASCD, 1989) and Stephen Covey (1991).

The ASCD list notes that effective school leaders do the following:

1. *They provide a sense of mission to their schools.* They demonstrate the ability to articulate what a school is supposed to do, particularly in terms of what it should do to benefit children.

2. *They engage in participative management.* They encourage a better organizational climate in a school by allowing teachers and staff to participate meaningfully in real decision making and not merely in efforts to "play at" getting people involved after decisions are already made.

3. *They provide support for instruction.* Instructional leaders are so committed to maintaining quality instruction as their primary organizational focus that when decisions must be made concerning priorities, instruction always comes first.

4. *They monitor instruction.* They know what is going on in the classrooms of their schools.

5. *They are resourceful.* Instructional leaders rarely allow circumstances in their organizations to get in the way of their vision for quality educational programs.

Stephen Covey has noted the following characteristics of what he refers to as "principle-centered leaders":

1. *They are continually learning.* Principle-centered people are constantly educated by their experiences.

2. *They are service oriented.* Those striving to be principle-centered leaders see life as a mission.

3. *They radiate positive energy.* Principle-centered people are cheerful, pleasant, and happy.

4. *They believe in other people.* Principle-centered people don't overreact to negative behaviors, criticisms, or human weaknesses.

5. *They lead balanced lives.* They read the best literature and magazines and keep up with current affairs and events.

6. *They see life as an adventure.* Principle-centered people savor life; they have no need to categorize or stereotype people and events.

7. *They are synergistic.* Principle-centered people serve as change catalysts in organizations, and they improve most situations in which they become involved.

8. *They exercise for self-renewal.* They regularly exercise the four dimensions of the human personality: physical, mental, emotional, and spiritual.

Another listing of critical leadership skills has been developed by the National Association of Elementary School Principals (NAESP, 1991). These skills are somewhat different from the ones you just reviewed. They are designed to enable school principals and assistant principals to review the skills they believe may need further refinement and improvement. As you consider each leadership area, take time to assess your own performance in this critical area of your work:

Area 1: Leadership Behavior

The assistant principal must:

1. Exercise vision and provide leadership that appropriately involves staff, students, and the community in the identification and accomplishment of the school's mission

2. Recognize the individual needs of all staff and students, including those who are at risk because of diverse cultures, backgrounds, and abilities

3. Apply effective human relations skills

4. Encourage and develop the leadership of others

5. Analyze relevant information, make decisions, delegate responsibility, and provide appropriate support and follow-up

6. Identify and creatively coordinate the use of available human, material, and financial resources to achieve the school's mission and goals

7. Explore, assess, develop, and implement educational concepts that enhance teaching and learning

8. Bond the school community through shared values and beliefs

9. Initiate and manage constructive change

10. Participate actively as a member of local, state, and national professional groups

Area 2: Communication Skills

The assistant principal must:

1. Articulate beliefs persuasively and effectively, defend decisions, explain innovations, and behave in ways that are congruent with these beliefs and decisions

2. Write clearly and concisely so that the message is understood by the intended audience

3. Use basic facts and data and recognize values when communicating priorities

4. Demonstrate skills in nonverbal communication, including personal impact, to communicate a positive image of the school

5. Use current technologies to communicate the school's philosophy, mission, needs, and accomplishments

6. Make effective use of mass media

7. Use active listening skills

8. Express disagreement without being disagreeable

9. Promote student and staff use of higher-level thinking skills

10. Exemplify the behavior expected of others

11. Keep communication flowing to and from the school

12. Communicate with the various constituencies within the school community

Area 3: Group Processes

The assistant principal must:

1. Apply the principles of group dynamics and facilitation skills

2. Involve staff, parents, students, and the community in setting goals

3. Resolve difficult situations by the use of conflict resolution skills

4. Match the appropriate decision-making techniques to the particular situation

5. Identify—in collaboration with staff, students, and parents—the decision-making procedures the school will follow

6. Apply the process of consensus building, both as a leader and as a member of a group

7. Achieve intended outcomes through the use of principles of motivation

In addition to these proficiencies related to the leadership responsibilities of school assistant principals, NAESP suggests that you may wish to review your performance in the following areas as well:

Supervisory Proficiencies

1. Curriculum

2. Instruction

3. Performance

4. Evaluation

Administrative and Management Competencies

1. Organizational management

2. Fiscal management

3. Political management

In addition to the various lists of leadership skills and attributes stated above, what are some items that you might list as characteristics of effective instructional leaders? _____

_____

_____

_____

_____

After considering the lists of leadership skills that you and others have generated, what are the areas in which you believe you have particular strengths at this time? _____

_____

_____

_____

_____

What skills do you believe you must develop? _____

_____

_____

_____

_____

Lists of leadership skills and competencies are appealing because they suggest that a person who knows and can demonstrate many of these individual characteristics is engaging in effective leadership behavior. Another perceived benefit of reviewing the proficiencies of NAESP or of ASCD's framework is that the reader can simply check these off as "present" or "not present." Unfortunately, leadership is a much more complex issue, and it is critical that you do not become complacent in your personal review by just looking over simplified lists of attributes. Engaging in that approach to the analysis of your leadership ability may be as naïve as claiming to be a chef after merely following recipes to produce a cake, soup, or whatever dish is outlined. It may be possible to say that someone who follows recipes has had success in cooking, but is he or she truly a chef?

ANOTHER APPROACH TO LEADERSHIP ANALYSIS

While individual authors and organizations have many very important specific issues that are believed to identify the characteristics of leaders, it is important to note that an effective leader is a person who is more than simply someone who can demonstrate most, if not all, the individual skills and attributes that are identified in one or another description of leadership skills. Returning again to the analogy of cooking, becoming a great chef is not simply the by-product of acquiring a huge collection of recipes that are drawn from dozens and dozens of existing cookbooks. Most diners realize that just knowing that a sauce contains one cup of this, one cup of that, and a pinch of spice stirred together and heated for an hour does not necessarily result in a fabulous dish. There is more involved.

The same is true of trying to understand and analyze the complex world of school leadership. The Association for Supervision and Curriculum Development notes that leaders are resourceful, they monitor instruction, they engage in participative management, and they provide a vision. Covey notes other attributes found in those who are perceived as effective leaders of organizations. These and many other perspectives are excellent resources that you may wish to consult. But reading, reviewing, or even memorizing any of these lists will never guarantee that you will be a true leader, either in your present role as an assistant principal or in any position you acquire in the future. You need to invest your own insights, experiences, and values to supplement the ingredients in the "recipes" offered by others. In short, it is a bit like the cook who believes it is possible to become a distinguished chef by merely following a book. There are many good cooks who never attain the status of renowned chef. And there are also great chefs who are not highly regarded because they know little about taking care of their kitchens. By the same token, there are individuals who are perceived as great visionary leaders who know next to nothing about what needs to be done to operate the organization each day, and there are great managers of the daily routines of a business without a sense of how these activities contribute to the achievement of great goals and vision. If you are to serve as a strong and effective leader, you cannot approach leadership by completing a checklist of attributes. Like a great chef, you need to invest your own perspectives, imagination, ideas, talents, and judgments into what constitutes the "proper balance" of ingredients, secret spices, cooking time, and the best possible presentation accompanied by the right wines.

SO WHAT *IS* EDUCATIONAL LEADERSHIP?

One way to begin to answer this critical question might be to use the cooking metaphor once again. After all, diners usually do not really care *how* a meal was prepared. Instead, they want to enjoy the product of the chef's creativity, hard work, and talent. The same is true of educational leadership. Not many are likely to identify excellence in a principal or assistant principal by reviewing several books on the attributes of leaders and deciding if the local school administrators parallel the books' descriptions.

The individual behavior of school leaders is not as important as what happens as a result of their work. In other words, another way to define the leadership that you should demonstrate in your current or future roles is by its outcome. Skills, proficiencies, and attributes are only tools to help achieve that end.

Consider some of the other broad, desirable outcomes for a school that is led by effective leaders:

- The school becomes a community where all members of the community work toward achieving common goals
- Students in the school achieve important personal and societal goals
- The school serves to prepare all students for important next steps in their personal and professional lives
- There is a shared sense of purpose achieved by all who are associated with the school as a community: administrators, teachers, staff, parents, community members, and most important, students
- The school activities and policies are derived as a result of the need to serve students

This list of possible desirable outcomes can continue for hundreds of additional statements. In the space below, add some of your own insights into the most important goals that should be achieved in a "good school." _____

_____

_____

_____

Now, select from the list of possible outcomes two or three goals that you believe are most important for your present school. For each goal, indicate the ways in which you believe you can be instrumental in moving your school toward the goal. What attributes, skills, or proficiencies must you possess or demonstrate to make the "good school" become a reality?

_____

_____

_____

_____

After you have prepared your statements of what you need in order to achieve your goals in leading a good school, think about two additional items. First, what is the timeline that you intend to follow in pursuing your professional development? If you are now just beginning the first year of your assistant principalship, what benchmarks do you intend to establish at intermediate times to judge your progress in achieving broad goals over an extended period of time? It is not likely that, as a first year school administrator, you will be able to create a schoolwide learning community in one year. But what steps leading to that broad objective are feasible in the near future? _____

_____

_____

_____

_____

A second issue should also be considered. Specifically, what other people do you need to consult, work with, or seek support from as you work toward achieving the goals you have set as effective leadership outcomes? Whose help do you need in preparing and presenting the "fabulous meal" that will serve as evidence of your excellence as a "chef"? In particular, how can you work effectively with your principal in achieving important goals for the school? And how can you assist the principal in achieving critical objectives? _____

_____

_____

_____

_____

YOUR PERSONAL PLAN

An assessment of your leadership skills early in your term as an assistant principal can serve as an important foundation for a personal portfolio and growth plan. This chapter included several different frameworks that have been developed to assist people in identifying critical attributes and competencies needed to lead schools. You may wish to consider these skills, or you may want to consider other issues that you will need to face in your role as an assistant principal. In particular, what do you believe should be the ultimate goals of effective leadership of your school? And how can you go about acquiring or refining your personal ability to become the kind of school leader who will be able to create the ideal school?

In the space below, identify some of your strengths and some of your limitations with regard to the leadership skills reviewed throughout this chapter. For each item, identify a timeline that you intend to follow in either strengthening that skill or finding ways to increase your personal skills. Note also some of the activities or strategies you believe may assist you in your improvement efforts. In addition, make certain to note the ways in which your principal may assist you in your effort to carry out your personal plan. _____

_____

_____

_____

_____

REFERENCES

Association for Supervision and Curriculum Development [ASCD]. (1989). *Instructional leadership* [Videotape]. Alexandria, VA: Author.

Covey, S. R. (1991). *Principle-centered leadership: Strategies for personal and professional effectiveness.* New York: Simon and Schuster.

National Association of Elementary School Principals [NAESP]. (1991). *Proficiencies for school principals* (Rev. ed.). Alexandria, VA: Author.

SUGGESTED ADDITIONAL READING

DePree, M. (1989). *Leadership is an art.* New York: Dell.

Heifetz, R. A. (1994). *Leadership without easy answers.* Cambridge, MA: Belknap Press of Harvard University Press.

Interstate School Leaders Licensure Consortium. (1996). *Standards for school leaders.* Washington, DC: Council of Chief State School Officers.

Maxwell, J. C. (1995). *Developing the leaders around you: How to help others reach their full potential.* Nashville, TN: Thomas Nelson.

National Association of Elementary School Principals. (2002). *Leading learning communities: Standards for what principals should know and be able to do.* Alexandria, VA: Author.

Wilmore, E. L. (2002). *Principal leadership: Applying the new Educational Leadership Constituent Council standards.* Thousand Oaks, CA: Corwin Press.

4

Carrying Out Your Management Duties

Roosevelt Clements was looking forward to this day. After eight years as a teacher in two different elementary schools in his district, and two and a half years of taking university courses required for a master's degree and state principal certification, he was now being asked to take on an assistant principalship at Carl Sandburg Elementary School. He would be working with an experienced principal, Janet Kilburn, and an equally seasoned teaching staff. Roosevelt had not visited the school before applying for an administrative position; he had met Janet only once at the selection interview; and he knew only one staff member, a third-grade teacher who had been a long-term substitute at one of the elementary schools where he had taught in the past. But the school had an excellent reputation. Sandburg students always scored well on the statewide achievement tests, and parents at the school were known around the city as a group that was highly involved in school projects. The school was located in a neighborhood where about half the students came from middle to upper middle-income households, and about half the pupils were residents of a low-income housing project. In short, this first administrative assignment was perfect in Roosevelt's mind. It was a great "launching pad" for his personal and professional goal of stepping into a principalship of his own within the next five years.

On the first day on the job, the principal invited her new assistant to start the day with a cup of coffee in her office. During this informal session, she invited Roosevelt to share some of his career objectives, and he responded that he wanted a principalship. "Based on what I know about you, that's certainly an achievable goal," noted Janet. "But I'll have to make certain that you are prepared by really learning the ropes during the next few years."

Roosevelt responded by beginning to list some of the ways he hoped to create a strong foundation so that he could be an effective instructional leader as a future principal. He noted how he wanted to be involved in curriculum development, instructional supervision, testing, and staff development. These were all things that he knew would be a big part of his future as a principal who really wanted to make a difference for children.

"Wow! I can't deny that those are really critical issues," said Janet. "I'll certainly get you involved in as many of these activities as I can. But don't forget, we also have a school to run here. How comfortable are you with the traditional 'Three B's of school administration—beans, busses, and budgets? You'll need to learn that a good principal has to handle the management of a school and be an effective instructional leader at the same time."

After a reflective pause, Roosevelt responded, "I guess I'd better get some experience in management and technical areas. I spent most of my time in graduate school learning about what they called the 'core areas' of research on instructional practices and learning theory."

The principal agreed that that information was certainly important, but she noted that there was also a lot more to do in order to be a really good principal. She suggested that they begin the new school year by laying out a framework of technical duties for the new assistant principal, showing times during the year when certain activities had to be addressed.

Roosevelt agreed. He knew that this was going to be a really great learning experience.

Roosevelt Clements has truly landed in what many might call a dream job. He was going to work in a nice school with a seasoned staff and an experienced and sympathetic principal. He knew that he had a lot to learn about many things if he was to land a principalship within the next few years, and his assignment to Carl Sandburg would be a good start for his very promising career.

What Mr. Clements will need to realize very quickly is that his path to the principalship will in many ways be paved by his ability to demonstrate that he can handle all the "little things" associated with managing a school. He can have a great vision for a school, show great dedication to the children, and have great intentions about what he would like to do as an outstanding instructional leader, but if he gets the reputation as a young administrator with "great ideas but no ability to conduct a meeting, set up a schedule, deal with special education, discipline students," and many similar tasks, he may stay in the assistant principal's office for a very long time.

This chapter is dedicated to helping you review some of the managerial and technical duties associated with your role as an assistant principal. As you read over the material presented here, you may wish to keep track of the things that you already know about, and also the areas where you will need to learn more. For example, you may have a good deal of past experience working with parents because you have been a coach who had to work with booster groups. Or, as a former counselor, you may already have some experience with student discipline, testing procedures, or scheduling. On the other hand, the importance of managing a school budget as the year progresses may be something that you were not exposed to in the past.

Not only do you need to assess your knowledge and skills associated with a variety of managerial tasks, you need to gain some insights into when different issues are likely to appear as priorities on your desk. In response to that, this chapter will highlight some likely issues that you will need to face before the year begins, at the start of the school year, during the year, and near the end of the school year. Even if you have to run to keep up with the demands of your new job for one year, perhaps you can begin to develop some personalized insights regarding which events are likely to appear in what order in the future.

You may enter the field of educational administration anticipating a new ability to truly serve as a leader by moving your school in new directions. New practices, staff development programs, goal setting, and many other things may be your dream. But as a beginning assistant, you also have to make certain that you "take care of business" right from the start. While maintaining your personal goals of leadership, you also need to focus on the technical aspects of running a school. This is a difficult challenge.

Unfortunately, a lot of beginning assistant principals are not as lucky as Roosevelt Clements was in the opening scenario. Often, people feel like they have been thrown into a situation where they need to spend all their time simply doing things that the principal does not want to do (or cannot do). They become accustomed to reacting to crises or at least to the next problem that finds them. They quickly fall into the trap of doing nothing more than responding to discipline referrals from teachers, soothing upset parents, and pinch-hitting for the principal when he or she is tied up with "more important matters." Behaving in this way will make your school year go quickly. After all, students are referred to your office all the time, parents are apt to walk into your office at all hours, and your principal is very busy. One school year follows another, and you can suddenly find yourself where many assistants do at a certain point in their careers: They have become excellent, skilled assistants, but they simply have not been successful in also learning all the other details that must be addressed in managing a school.

Although effective instructional leadership should be the ultimate goal of any educational leader, the management side of an assistant principal's job is also extremely important. In fact, assistant principals are often judged as appropriate candidates by others for future administrative jobs largely in terms of their ability to carry out managerial duties. This chapter is written for you if you are not as fortunate as Roosevelt Clements, who has a great mentor in his principal, Janet Kilburn. It includes a review of traditional tasks required of assistant principals as ongoing activities. After the responsibilities that tend to be part of your ongoing duties are considered, we will look at different times during a typical school year to determine responsibilities that need to be addressed at those times. As we look at these various duties, you should rate your personal competence in engaging in these different areas.

APPARENT CONTRADICTIONS

The most critical skills that must be mastered by any beginning assistant principal concern developing an appreciation for personal values and beliefs, as noted in Chapter 2. As a result, this chapter might seem contradictory, because it looks at the important areas of technical and managerial skills needed for assistant principals to succeed in their jobs. People often speak of administrative skills in an almost negative way, as if these kinds of things are below the dignity of a true leader's concern. The implication is that being an effective school leader is something well beyond mere management.

This chapter looks at the technical and managerial side of the assistant principal's job. The goal here is to present an overview of the many tasks that need to be done each year by school assistant principals, and to work with you to set up a schedule for carrying out these tasks. Some of the items might be classified as formal or mandated activities that are required by state law, collective bargaining agreements, or local school board policy. Exact dates will vary in different school districts or states. Other important technical duties need to be done by effective assistant principals, even if they are not officially required.

FORMAL REQUIREMENTS

As a school administrator, you must do a number of things each year because they are formal requirements of the job. If you miss the deadlines associated with these tasks, you may be in violation of labor contracts, local policies, or even state or local laws. As an assistant principal, you could lose your job or be held personally and legally liable if you do not meet these deadlines and due dates. Or, you could cause your principal significant problems; your supervising administrator is accountable for your actions.

Deadlines are important, but they are often listed in formal memos, the district's weekly calendar of events, job descriptions, school board policies, and a wide array of other places that make them relatively hard to ignore. Few assistant principals or principals are wholly unprepared for the fact that, for example, they must complete the evaluations of untenured teachers in their buildings by a certain prescribed date. This is an important technical or managerial task that you must address, but it is not usually a subtle issue that is easy to forget.

INFORMAL TASKS

Informal tasks are extremely important but differ from the activities required by law or policy. These are the duties that you will not necessarily find listed in the local district policy manual, or in the school code for your state, or even in terms of the negotiated contract for your local teachers' association. However, failure to do some of these things might make a difference in how you are able to carry out your job as an administrator. They are the kinds of things that make your school run a bit more smoothly and reduce tensions and frustrations, not only for you but also for your staff, students, the community with whom you work, and above all for your principal.

The next few pages will list some of the important things—both formal and informal—that need to be done during the school year. The lists indicate activities that are likely to be part of your duties all year, and also things that are ordinarily issues needing attention before the year begins, during the year, and toward the end of the school year to ensure that next year will be easier than this one.

THROUGHOUT THE YEAR

Before going too much farther with this review of managerial tasks that you will need to address throughout the school year, it should be noted that everything that you do as an assistant principal must be defined and specified by your principal. When it comes to an issue such as "What do I do and when do I do it?" it is truly a call that is to be made by your supervisor.

Having made that observation, you can probably assume that three assignments will be delegated to you and most other assistant principals across the country. One is student discipline, another is the oversight of special education, and the third is supervising the attendance reporting and monitoring procedures in your school. Of course, this may differ from case to case and school to school. For example, where there are schools with multiple assistants, as is true of many high schools, it is likely that some ongoing duties will be assigned to certain individuals on a regular basis. Only one of the three or four assistants in a large secondary school may be in charge of special education programs. On the other hand, it is rare to find any school where any assistant is not involved with student discipline. Another variable that will likely affect your duties is the background and personal preferences of your principal. A principal who has extensive experience in special education may prefer to work directly with students in that area. And, in some cases, principals enjoy working with discipline because it enables them to continue to have regular contact with students.

Regardless of possible exceptions, assistants are often frontline decision makers in student discipline and special education. The practice followed in most schools is for teachers who are unable to handle unruly students in their classrooms to refer them to the school administration ("Go to the office!") for discipline. In schools with assistants, this means that these students will arrive in your office at some point in the school day.

Discipline. Many assistant principals take their first jobs as administrators fully aware of the fact that a major responsibility that will face them involves the need to discipline students. Some may look at this duty as something that is anything but desirable. But disciplining students is truly an instructional activity. First, keep in mind that your job as a school administrator is always to do whatever you can to ensure that the instructional programs of students are not impeded, and classrooms with disruptions caused by misbehaving students will not be effective learning environments. It may sound a bit like rationalization, but you are a critical part of the instructional team at your school when you are able to assist teachers by working with particular problem students.

Also, it is worthwhile remembering that discipline is best understood not as punishment, but rather as a form of counseling and student advisement. While certainly not always the case, it is also true that students who act in inappropriate ways at school are often individuals who have a variety of personal or emotional problems in their lives. As a result, being "sent to the office" may be an extremely positive event in the lives of some individuals. It may be that the time you spend with a student in your office as a discipline referral can actually be a turning point in a young person's life. Schooling is an opportunity to learn in a variety of settings, and your office can become a place where important lessons are presented. A discipline hearing can be a rare time when the opportunity exists for the student to talk to an adult on a one-to-one basis. As many educators know, disruptive behavior is often an effort by students to gain attention and recognition because they are being ignored by others. Spending time with a responsible adult may be an extremely important event for a child. In recent years, there has been a steady increase in the number of school guidance counselors who have opted to move from their original offices into administration because they actually do more management (test administration, scheduling, etc.) than they do student counseling. Being an assistant principal is often a way to return to their original career focus of helping students.

As with so many issues encountered by school leaders, your approach and perspectives on the importance of student discipline as a major part of your duties as an assistant principal will depend on your individual point of view and educational platform, as we discussed in Chapter 2. In the space provided below, note your personal stance regarding the value of

having effective student discipline skills in your role as a beginning
educational leader. _____

_____

_____

_____

_____

Regardless of whether you see maintaining student discipline as a
good or a bad feature of your job, it is what you will be called upon to do
as an assistant principal. Therefore, you will need to be sure that you can
carry out this responsibility effectively and efficiently. Make certain to
do several things when you walk into a school. First, make sure to learn
the school district's code of conduct. Pay particular attention to the classification of offenses, if that is part of the document. What are considered
"major infractions" that require notification and conferencing with
parents? What will automatically result in in-school or out-of-school suspension? Are there behaviors that must be reported either to local district
authorities or even to the police? You need to know this information when
you consider the actions of students who are sent to you.

Talk with your principal about his or her views on student discipline.
In these days when so many schools have adopted "zero tolerance" policies
about practices by students, you need to recognize what your supervisor's
views are before you act. Is a nail file brought to school by an eighth grader
the same as a high school student bringing a knife on campus? And what
will you do in the event that a ninth-grade girl is seen taking an aspirin
in the cafeteria? Newspaper headlines are often the result of such events
being viewed as "overkill" reactions in local schools. Make certain that
you know what your boss's views are likely to be.

Finally, be attentive to your individual school's perspectives on
effective discipline. In many cases, parents have worked with teachers,
administrators, and even students to devise a code of conduct that is
unique to a school. It would be a huge mistake to ignore this collective
vision of what is or is not acceptable in the school in which you now work.
Your individual judgment regarding the acceptability of certain student
behaviors must take a backseat to the views of others. Do your homework.

What are some additional ways in which you may gain insights into
the expectations for discipline that may be present in your school? _____

_____

_____

_____

_____

Special Education. With little doubt, another area in which you will be called
upon to serve as an assistant to your principal is in the area of special
education. Specifically, you will probably be called upon through the
school year to serve as the administrative representative in two cases.

One is in the area of Section 504 Conferencing (i.e., as part of the requirement for accommodations for students with special learning needs identified in Section 504 of the Handicapped Accommodations federal law of 1973). The second is in the area of serving as the administrator who will work with parents and professionals involved in the development of Individualized Educational Programs (IEPs) for students with learning or physical disabilities, or both.

In 504 Conferences, it will be your dual role to speak on behalf of both the student's needs and the abilities of the school to meet the realistic demands of the individual student. This is often a challenging and stressful role. On the one hand, you are expected to find ways to ensure that reasonable accommodations can be made for any student with identified needs to be able to work effectively in a school environment. This may mean simply making certain that a student with limited distance vision is always assigned a seat in the front of a classroom in order to be able to see the teacher's presentation on a chalkboard or see audiovisual materials clearly. It may also involve the need to provide electronic devices to enable a child with a diagnosed hearing deficit to understand what is taking place in classes. On the other hand, serving as a representative of the school or district may place you in conflicting situations at times. There have been numerous cases where "reasonable accommodations" for students are defined in somewhat unreasonable ways by parents. For example, is a child who feels threatened by other youngsters on a school bus able to seek roundtrip individual taxi service back and forth to school each day? What about a child who is very shy being provided a personal, private bathroom throughout the day? Your responsibility must be to think of a child's needs, of course. But as a school administrator, you must also consider the financial impact some requests or demands are likely to have on the limited resources of your school or district.

If you have already been involved in 504 Conferences (either as an administrator or in your "past life" as a counselor or teacher), what are some of the specific demands that have been made in the name of students? How have you been able to address these expectations? _____

_____

_____

_____

_____

Serving as the administrative representative to committees initiated to develop IEPs for special needs students can also be a challenge that at times requires you to switch between serving as a student advocate and a school manager. Your sense of dedication to learners will no doubt make you supportive of students, parents, and special education advocates who want to ensure that the child in question is provided with a plan of studies that will allow for individual success. Taking a remedial mathematics class, receiving special tutoring in reading, or many similar suggested strategies are not particularly difficult approaches that may be requested.

However, requiring a teacher to spend enormous amounts of individual time with a single student may be something that seemingly "makes sense" for the student, but the teacher involved may not be terribly pleased with the recommendation. Remember that the conferences that specify the nature of an IEP are meant to be opportunities for several different parties to reach a consensus on how best to serve the student who needs special attention. Your job, in large measure, is to serve as a mediator in a complex and often emotional process. Be aware, too, that this kind of activity is often very time-consuming. An IEP conference may take anywhere from an hour to most of a day to complete. At the same time, you are also responsible for dealing with a stack of discipline referrals on your desk, or the need to observe teachers' classes, and a wide variety of other duties that you have as an assistant principal.

Indicate ways in which you may have already been involved in IEP planning and conferencing, on "either side of the desk." How will you apply your past experience to this responsibility as an assistant principal?

_____

_____

_____

_____

_____

If you do not have a background in the area of special education, it is critical that you acquire knowledge and insights into this very important area of your school. Read journals, take a university course on special education, talk with special education teachers in your school, and make certain to form a working relationship with the director of pupil services or special education administrator for your district. Again, make it a point to keep your principal informed as to issues that have appeared in your conferencing with people related to special education issues and practices in the school.

Attendance. Attendance is another area in which you are likely to be assigned continuing responsibility throughout each school year. Again, this can be viewed as a time-consuming and even aggravating duty that hardly seems related to the world of instructional leadership. Yet while it may appear that there are more important things to do besides serving as an attendance clerk each day, this job deserves better appreciation.

First, overseeing attendance for a school is an important contribution to the instructional program of your school. It may seem simplistic, but the fact of the matter is that students are not likely to learn if they do not attend school regularly. You are a major contributor to the learning of any student when you do your part to increase the likelihood that students are in attendance each day.

The second reason for being concerned about good attendance in your school is that doing so will have a direct, positive impact on the school's overall program. Tax money, whether local or state, comes to your school based on a very simple concept: Money follows students. When they attend school, you get paid money to operate your programs. Average Daily Attendance (ADA) figures drive most funding programs across the nation. That is why it is so critical for individual schools to present accurate and timely reports of attendance each day. If you have been designated as the assistant responsible for managing attendance, you are able to make a major contribution to your school's ability to carry out its programs. Whether your primary concern is to ensure that students attend classes so that they are able to learn each day, or because you want to make certain that funds are provided to your campus, attendance oversight is an important duty.

In order to understand more completely the ways in which attendance management is important, make certain that you spend time talking with whomever on your staff (e.g., the school attendance clerk, registrar, head secretary, etc.) is the "frontline person" responsible for collecting attendance data each day. Learn answers to the following issues as a way to appreciate the importance of this administrative duty:

At what time each day does district policy or state law specify that a student must be considered "absent"? _____

_____

_____

How many absences during a marking period, semester, or school year constitute "chronic absenteeism" on the part of a student? _____

_____

_____

What reports must be filed with the district office of pupil personnel services to report students who are identified as "chronic absentees"? ____

_____

_____

What are the legal remedies that may be used to enforce school attendance policies? _____

_____

What are the steps followed each day, each term, or each marking period by your in-school attendance clerk in reporting to the school district?

_____

_____

_____

_____

PLANNING FOR THE SCHOOL YEAR

While the issues of student discipline, special education, and attendance management may be ongoing duties assigned to you all year long, there will be other things that will likely cross your desk throughout the year. In preparation for these matters, you can take some steps to get ready for an effective first year by looking at activities that you may carry out at specific times.

BEFORE THE YEAR BEGINS

Many people get their first assistant principalship during the summer, before the new school year begins. In an ideal world, you might be selected as an assistant in May or June, with the understanding that your contract officially begins on July 1 and that teachers will be back by early August, two or three weeks before students arrive. In that imaginary, ideal world you might have several weeks or a few months to plan for the next year; check over the school; learn about the students, teachers, staff, community, and school district; and so on. In the real world, however, you might get your first assignment as an assistant principal only a few weeks (or days) before the school year begins. Or you might get a call to take on a new job in the middle of a school year.

Regardless of the situation in which you find yourself, you can do a number of things in the months, weeks, or even days before teachers and students walk into your school. These activities are classified into several areas: building preparation; materials and supplies; communications with staff, students, and parents; and finally, perhaps most critical, personal preparation.

The following activities might help you to prepare for your first year as an assistant principal, especially if you have never worked in this particular school in the past.

Building Preparation Activities

- Walk around the school with your principal and the chief custodian to learn as much as you can about the location and operation of significant features of the school building. For example, where are all the storage rooms and closets, fire extinguishers, emergency lighting and alarm controls, telephones, and any other similar items that you may need to make use of in emergencies or during the course of any school day?
- Learn how to use the public address system for the school; practice making announcements while no one is in the building.
- Spend time with your principal learning any special codes that might be necessary for communication during emergency or crisis situations. For example, some schools have adopted a policy of announcing something like, "Mr. Jones is in the building" to alert teachers and staff that a bomb threat has been received, but without alarming students immediately. Additional codes might exist to alert people that an intruder is in the school, or that students must be kept in their classrooms because a weapon was discovered on campus.

- Learn how to operate, override, or even disconnect the building's fire alarm system or security systems in case that should become necessary.
- Review the school building evacuation plan.
- Check over the school's book room, vault, and supply closets, and inventory books and supplies to ensure that the school year will begin with a sufficient stock of all necessary materials.
- Walk around the outside of your school during the summer months to inspect its external conditions. Report any areas needing attention to your principal. Remember that the outside of your building, including the grounds around it, is what taxpayers and the public see every day.
- Learn about your building's idiosyncrasies, hidden rooms, and so forth. (This is particularly an adventure in older buildings or in areas where several wings have been added over the years. Often, you will find small closets in gyms, auditoriums, and other similar areas of the school).
- If your school must make use of portable classrooms because of overcrowding, learn the location of the units so that you can proceed to any trouble spots without consulting a "road map."
- Since a major part of your duties will be related to student discipline, check with your principal to see if it would be acceptable to contact your district's security office or local police department and have them lead you through a security and safety audit of your campus.
- Arrange your office so it reflects you and your personal style; move the desk, put up photos and plants, and so on. (This may seem like an unimportant thing, but your personal workspace really tells people a lot about you very quickly).

Materials and Supplies

- Review supplies and inventory procedures for the school.
- Make certain that you have an ample supply of forms (e.g., leave request forms, insurance forms, discipline referral forms) on hand to start the school year.
- Talk with your principal and make certain that such things as student and staff handbooks are ready for distribution as soon as the school year begins.
- Arrange the book room in a way that makes sense to you if your duties involve monitoring the textbook distribution process for the school.

Communication With Staff, Parents, and Students

- Listen and learn as much as you can about the local culture of the school, your neighborhood, and the school district. Who are some of the local heroes? Are there any legends to learn? (Even if you come to this school from another building in the district, this is an important step if you want to "hit the ground running" and know what is taking place in this school.)

- Work with your principal and other experienced personnel to identify important local community groups, individuals, or organizations.
- Meet and introduce yourself to as many individual teachers as possible as they stop in at the school before going back on duty.
- Read local newspapers; subscribe to one if you live in another community.
- Spend time with the office staff; get to know their personalities and preferences regarding such things as how they prefer to be addressed. (Is it "Mrs. Smith," or can you simply say "Mary"?)

Curriculum

- Learn the teaching culture of the school. Are teams used? Are there teachers who have a reputation for always excelling as loners? Who might work well with whom?
- Review the district curriculum guide and graded course of study.
- Learn about special education or inclusion programs that are followed in the district, and consider the implications for your role in the school.
- Schedule a time to confer with the principal about additional specifics of curriculum planning and development that are related to the vision for this school.

Personal Preparation

- Read journals that you may previously have put aside to learn about major educational trends that are likely to face you as a school leader.
- Talk to people to learn about special school traditions, events, and customs.
- Learn how to use your two-way radio.
- Set up a tentative monthly schedule of events for the coming year. Set up a tickler file system to remind you of significant deadlines that you will need to meet.
- Set up your personal phone filing system on your desk; program speed dials for frequently called telephone numbers; set up your e-mail account and system.
- Schedule some time to talk with your principal about his or her expectations for your work as an assistant this year. Express some of the personal and professional goals that you hope to address.
- Review district policy manuals to learn about attendance reporting procedures, disciplinary policies, and other information that will likely be a part of the duties that are assigned to you in your role as an assistant principal.

AFTER THE YEAR STARTS

No matter how well you plan your next year, you will quickly learn that, as an assistant principal, you will be expected to react to issues and problems rather than engage in a great deal of proactive, planned behavior. Nevertheless, it is possible to anticipate some major events. Some of these will take place at the beginning of the year, and some will come later. Be prepared as well as you can.

Building and Physical Plant Activities

- Keep your eyes open for any unusual signs of wear and tear in the building, particularly as these might be related to the health and safety of students and staff.
- Work with your principal in learning how and when to carry out fire drills, tornado drills, and other forms of disaster drills as required by local laws and school district policy.
- Keep an eye on graffiti and vandalism around the school and make certain that, wherever possible, these problems are taken care of quickly; do not let your school walls and property become a place where graffiti and tagging are acceptable.

Materials and Supplies

- Make certain that supplies ordered during the summer arrive.
- Distribute textbooks in a manner described by past practice in this school or consistent with textbook distribution policy of the school district.
- Oversee the use of consumable supplies throughout the building (e.g., chalk, paper) to prevent an interruption in needed material in the middle of the school year.

Communication With Staff, Students, and Parents

- Work with your principal to plan parent meeting dates for the year with your staff, PTA or PTO, booster clubs, and so forth.
- While attending any parent or community functions at the school, make a special effort to introduce yourself personally to as many people as possible. Hand out business cards with your phone number and e-mail address.
- Carry out all supervisory duties of events and activities as assigned to you by your principal.
- Visit as many classes as possible.
- Keep a record of discipline referrals; maintain a record of decisions and recommendations that are made during disciplinary meetings; communicate with parents as necessary concerning disciplinary infractions.

- Learn the culture of the school as it relates to formal and informal observations of holidays and other events.
- Communicate as necessary with parents concerning patterns of excessive student absences.
- Call parents of exceptionally good students periodically to let them (students and parents) know that their positive behavior is worthy of note.

System Responsibilities

- Learn the mandated census dates for your state (i.e., the official date on which enrollment must be reported to the district and the state educational agency).
- Work with your principal so that you can learn procedures associated with building your school's budget for the next year.
- Learn what is required and gather data systematically and continuously for the school's annual report, which will have to be submitted to the central office at some point toward the end of the current school year.
- Systematically document your personal and professional accomplishments.
- Make certain to learn and meet all deadlines for the completion of important tasks such as the evaluation of untenured teachers, first-year teachers, tenured faculty, and classified staff, and the supervision of activities and athletic programs, planning for substitute teachers, and so on.

TOWARD THE END OF THE YEAR

The last few months and weeks of every school year are a big part of your job, because many annual events pile up and you need to make certain that they are completed in a timely fashion.

Building Maintenance

- Check with teachers and other staff members to gather input regarding modifications that might be needed in classrooms, offices, and elsewhere around the building. Report this information to your principal.

Instructional Materials

- Learn how textbooks distributed at the beginning of the school year are accounted for, collected, and stored. Carry out the collection of books; follow through with notices to parents about lost or damaged books.

Communication With Teachers, Students, and Parents

- Submit your annual report to the principal.
- Share with staff members strategies or techniques that might be helpful in the improvement of school practice.
- Hold additional discussions with parents of students who have had a particularly difficult year because of either disciplinary problems or academic difficulties. You cannot always require parents to attend such additional meetings, but the open invitation to spend time discussing any concerns about a student's progress may be a most welcome opportunity for some.
- Spend some extra time with students who have been frequent visitors to your office for disciplinary issues during the past year. These need not be formal conferences; brief informal chats in the hallways or between classes are an effective way to let students appreciate that you still have an interest in their progress.

General Management

- Work with the principal in planning the school's master schedule for next year.
- Discuss with the principal the planning and coordination of such normal spring activities as the spring student play, prom, field day, sporting events, graduation ceremonies, and so forth.

A couple of observations about this list are important. First, remember that your primary duty always is to assist your principal. Therefore, nothing said here should suggest that you do anything without the approval of your principal. Second, the list of activities and duties is not exhaustive. It certainly does not include all that you do or that you might do. Undoubtedly, you and your principal are likely to identify other important activities for your school. Third, no priorities are suggested. You and your supervisor must make your own determination of what tasks must be done first. It is a critical decision to make, but not on your own.

BUILDING A PERSONAL PLAN

This chapter dealt with a review of many of the important technical and managerial skills that a new assistant principal needs to master on the way to becoming an effective and proactive educational leader. There was recognition that, among other issues, you will no doubt be responsible for the oversight of three important areas: student discipline, special education, and attendance. We also considered a number of tasks as possible activities to carry out before the school year begins, after the year has started, and in preparation for the closing of the school year. You should not become overwhelmed with the responsibilities of your job. This chapter alerts you to develop an understanding of major issues that need to be addressed in a systematic way.

On the last few pages consider your own situation and identify some tasks that you will need to address throughout the school year. In listing the specific tasks, make sure that you do so according to a priority. Another issue that you will certainly have to deal with throughout your administrative career is effective time management. You will find numerous books and experts available to consult in this area, but really, time management means nothing more than making a decision about what must be attended to first. As a result, if you plan to attack several issues throughout the school year, begin here in your management of your time by asking, "What comes first?" After you decide the answer to that question, you may also want to identify specific strategies for carrying out your many duties according to a reasonable schedule.

Before the Year Begins

_____

_____

_____

_____

After the School Year Is Under Way

_____

_____

_____

_____

In Preparation for the End of the Year

_____

_____

_____

_____

Remember that no matter how well you plan your year, you will encounter surprises and unplanned events, or you may discover some assigned responsibilities for which you do not feel well prepared. Always remember that you will never be able to stand totally alone and be effective. Talk to your principal, call other assistants in your district, and gather input from your teachers, secretarial and custodial staff, parents, and others. After all, you will get a lot more accomplished when you work as part of a team.

5

Cool
Your Ego

Gabe Carter had spent nearly three years completing his master's degree in educational administration at State University while working full-time as a teacher in the Grange City Schools. It was not an easy road to follow at times. As a varsity basketball coach, he was not able to take classes on Tuesday nights. Family responsibilities and financial limitations made it difficult for him to take more than two classes at any time. He had to give up any summer vacations for two years. But now he had his degree and he also had qualified for a provisional principal certificate for his state. Soon he received word that the Grange City Schools had an opening for an assistant principal at Groveville Middle School.

Gabe was very happy to get an administrative position after all of his sacrifices to finish the university's program. He looked forward to going to Groveville where the principal, Marie Swenson, was known to be one of the toughest and most demanding administrators in the district. Gabe wanted to learn as much as he could about being an effective school administrator, and he knew that spending time with Marie would be a great way to learn from someone with really high expectations.

Not long after he started at Groveville, Gabe began to see why Marie had the reputation that she did. From his first day on the job, she began to assign Gabe a wide array of duties, many of which did not strike the new assistant as particularly "glamorous." He was aware that one of the traditional duties of any assistant involved the oversight of textbooks for the school. Marie informed Gabe that he not only would be responsible for distributing (and collecting) the books, but he would also be expected to keep the textbook storage room clean and well organized. Gabe had come to work his first day with a freshly cleaned suit and new shirt and tie, but after a few hours in the book room, he vowed to come to work the next day in jeans and a sweatshirt. After the bookroom was organized, Marie told Gabe that he would be the school's representative at truancy court whenever a student from Groveville was summoned to attend. Gabe remembered hearing from other assistant principals over the years how being the truancy court rep meant spending hours in a dimly lit courtroom waiting for cases to appear before the bench. And it also meant a lot of tension and conflict with parents, the students, and, at times, the truancy court judge. By now, it was also clear that Marie intended for Gabe to be the first line of defense for any discipline cases in the school. That meant that many days would involve only disciplining students or engaging in lengthy hearings with parents. In addition to these responsibilities, Gabe was also aware that he had to do many other things as assistant principal, including evaluating teachers, managing a part of the building budget, going to meetings at the central office, providing coverage in the evenings and on weekends for sporting events and other school activities, and many other "duties assigned by the principal of the school."

Gabe initially became interested in school administration for two reasons. First, we wanted to increase his salary. Second, and even more important, he wanted to have a greater impact on students than he had in his former positions as classroom teacher and coach. Now he was learning that he appeared to be serving as a gofer for a principal who often did not seem to respect his abilities to do more than intervene in discipline cases or chase after lost textbooks.

If you were to provide some feedback to Gabe at this point in his career, what might you suggest? _____

_____

_____

_____

_____

As we noted in the first chapter, being an assistant principal is not always a glamorous educational job. In fact, there are times when it may seem to you that it is not even truly a leadership position in education. Much of your time is spent reacting to people and situations. Teachers expect you to carry their concerns "up to the principal" while you still remain loyal to those who are working in classrooms. Your principal expects loyalty and willingness to do whatever duties deemed necessary. All of this may seem to be contradictory to your initial image of what being a leader is supposed to be about. Frustration often mounts as the hours available in a day to accomplish everything that you want to do and are asked to do by others begin to dwindle.

This chapter is meant to help you understand your role more completely as a responder to the expectations of others. No doubt you are a bright, capable, energetic, and ambitious educator. Now, you are an assistant principal, and like Gabe Carter you find yourself in a school administration job in which you get some of the most challenging duties imaginable. You are the person who listens to complaints. You deal with most of the student discipline problems in your school. Often, you are the person who is assigned the task of contacting parents about problems with their child's behavior, low test scores, or many other issues that are often really quite unpleasant. While you take care of these things happening in your school, the principal seems to get most of the credit—even though you, the teachers, and the staff did all the work. But the fact is, the principal may get credit when things go well but also get the blame when things do not go as planned.

MAINTAINING YOUR BALANCE AND PERSPECTIVE

The issue to be considered here is really that of helping you to retain your perspective. On the one hand, you are an adult, possibly a successful parent, established in your community, with years of experience as an effective and well-respected professional educator. You have several hundred or even thousands of former students who see you as a major force in their lives. In short, you truly are a person deserving respect, and you should be shown dignity and be held in high regard.

On the other hand, you are a "new kid on the block" professionally. You are serving as an assistant principal, a job traditionally understood as the starting point in a career as an educational leader. Because of your former professional experiences in the classroom, you have decided to work toward having a similar impact on a school or even a school district. But now you are at a new beginning in your professional life. No matter how many years of experience you may have as a classroom teacher, counselor, or coach, you are now a rookie. Where you served as a mentor to others last year, you now sometimes need a mentor to find your own way.

This type of sudden role shift is often very difficult for people to handle. It is difficult to accept a new, lower status after being so highly regarded in the recent past. Your job is not about feeding your ego: It is about improving the education of children. Being an assistant principal is often a real test of a person's ability to demonstrate humility. You have not been hired to be a "coprincipal" or "senior advisor." You are *an assistant to the person in charge.*

So what can you do to maintain your sense of accomplishment while also learning a new job? The secret may quite simply be found in your skill at maintaining a balance between keeping your mind focused on what you were while striving to become more. A first step in that process can be taking a look at yourself in terms of the specific skills that you believe you bring to your new job, and also some of the areas in which you know you need to increase basic understanding.

List three to five skills, insights, or special talents that you have had as an educator and that you believe are important personal contributions to your ability to serve as an assistant principal. (For example, do you have strong interpersonal skills that will help you in dealing with conflict with students, parents, staff, or others?) _____

_____

_____

_____

_____

What are some areas in which you believe you need to gain additional skill or competence during your time as an assistant principal. (Perhaps you are not a "detail person.") _____

_____

_____

_____

_____

TALK WITH YOUR PRINCIPAL

Many principals schedule a specific time each week to meet with their assistant principals. During these sessions, campus leaders can talk about major events that are going to take place in school (e.g., statewide achievement testing, scheduling for the next semester, campus career days, etc.) and who is responsible for what during those times. These meetings also form the basis of assigning after-school supervisory duties for sports events, plays, "meet the teacher" nights, and all the different things that take place in a school. It can be a time when you can open conversations with your principal along the lines of identifying some of the ways in which you can learn more about balancing your personal and professional strengths and limitations. Remember that, for the most part, you were hired as an assistant principal largely because of your potential to do a complex job. Unless you happen to have worked with your principal in some other capacities over the years, the two of you may be coworkers who really do not know that much about each other. Therefore, spending a few minutes every once in a while talking about talents that you may have (or limitations that you possess) may be a way to enable your "boss" to begin looking at you in less limited terms.

Consider, for example, an assistant principal who has been very involved with a lot of community development projects in the neighborhood in which the school is located. It is quite possible that all the principal knows about the assistant is his or her years of teaching experience. If the principal expresses a need for the school to engage in more outreach activities in its surrounding community, this could be an excellent time for the assistant to step forward and reveal any "hidden" talents. In this way, there can be a gradual shifting from being seen as an assistant principal to being seen as a very valuable member of a school's leadership team.

What are some your personal or professional skills that you may wish to share with your principal so you can increasingly be seen as a stronger contributor to your school's success? _____

_____

_____

_____

_____

COUNT TO TEN . . . AGAIN AND AGAIN

Of course, you may not be blessed with an opportunity to work with a principal who is even remotely interested in getting to know you or your special potential contributions to the school. Not every principal of every school is a great leader. Simply stated, this is a place where you will truly earn a future positive reputation by being able to work effectively with a person who is known to do nothing to help assistants.

When you are at a point where you are truly frustrated with how you feel you are being treated, the first choice of behavior would, of course, be being able to discuss your concerns directly with your principal so that the two of you can come to an agreement regarding your role. That would be an approach to follow in the ideal world. But sometimes circumstances make an ideal practice impossible. If you realize that you will never be recognized as a true professional and you cannot confront this concern through a conversation with the principal, you have three basic choices. One is to march into your principal's office and demand not to be treated as a lackey or doormat. Assert yourself! You may feel very good about this choice for a few minutes or even days. After all, you stood up for your rights and took no grief from someone who obviously did not respect you. Of course, your sense of satisfaction will begin to wane as soon as you hear reports that your principal told other principals in the district or in surrounding districts about how "that new hothead assistant principal came in screaming about not liking to be ordered around so much!" To put it very mildly, this episode will not stand out as a major high point in your career. In fact, just one outburst may brand you as a bad colleague forever.

When you feel as if you are not being respected by your principal, you have another choice. You can get in touch with your district office of human resources and begin looking around for another assistant principalship in another school where the principal might be much more sympathetic to your wants and needs. If you take this route, be prepared for a couple of predictable responses. First, human resource directors have a fairly standard question when asked about transfers: "Why do you want to leave your present school?" Keep in mind at this point that you do not want to break one of the cardinal rules for anyone seeking a job: Never badmouth your present employer. Doing so will almost surely brand you as a malcontent, a troublemaker, a whiner, or (see the previous paragraph) "a hothead who is not a team player." You may actually get the transfer that you are seeking, but you may soon wake up to discover that bridges are now burning behind you and that you have just joined the ranks of lifelong assistant principals, even if that was not your career goal.

So the first two options may not appeal to you. Here is a third choice, but it will not make you very happy at first. It will not bring about a change (as in seeking a transfer), and it may not make you feel as good as being able to blow off some steam by screaming at the boss.

This option may ensure that you will enjoy a somewhat more successful administrative career, however. Continue to do your job as effectively as you can and learn how to live with what you believe are the challenges to your professionalism. Consider a very important question: Does anything that you are now being asked to do have a serious negative impact on your long-term and short-term career goals? _____

_____

_____

_____

_____

If the answer to the previous question is basically "No," you may wish to balance your personal sense of anger or hurt by thinking about the need to restrict your own sense of self-importance a bit. When Gabe Carter in the opening scenario was put in charge of the school's book room, it was clearly a job that he believed was not consistent with what he thought an educational leader had to perform. His view was that a future principal needed to be learning about much more important things. Besides that, he was dressed as a professional and he was not ready to climb around on dirty shelving units in a storage room. Fortunately, Gabe did not start his career by confronting his principal over this perceived limitation to his duties, and he did not contact the personnel office to seek a transfer. In either case, his actions probably would not have changed the views of his principal, who saw the organization of the book room as a job appropriate for her assistant. Besides that, Principal Swenson had had to do the exact same job when she was an assistant principal a few years back. In addition, what's so undignified about the job of taking care of the school's textbooks? Gabe might now need to rethink his assumptions about the real job of being a school administrator. From the perspective of the principal, being asked to do some jobs is not meant as an insult to a person's professionalism. Rather, they are normal parts of a job that will be anything but glamorous at times.

Another tip that you may wish to consider when faced with tasks that at first might not seem to be consistent with your new status as an administrator is always to think of what you are learning. Gabe did not really think that sitting around at truancy court all afternoon was a valuable use of time. But spending his time in that way was surely something that could give him some rather important insights into not only how the law worked, but more important, why it is so critical to enforce attendance policies in the first place. Truancy proceedings are normally instances when the courts are focused on supporting education by ensuring that students are in school. They are not meant as punitive events.

CLOSING THOUGHTS

The final word of advice offered here is found in the title of this chapter: Cool Your Ego. You will do a lot to increase both your personal learning about your new job and your status in the eyes of those around you who are looking at your daily performance as a school administrator. You need to guard against feeling like a victim, even when you believe that you are doing all the work while someone else gets the credit. You cannot feel sorry for yourself. The position that you hold is that of *assistant* principal. Although this obvious statement may shock or even insult you at first, you are not hired to be a lead administrator—yet. Your job is carefully defined as that of assisting the lead administrator. This means, perhaps more than anything else, that you need to rein in your understandable pride and ego. Again, you were hired because you demonstrated more leadership and managerial skills than others who applied for your position—didn't you?

The fact is that you were most likely hired because you appeared to have the potential of adding your unique skills to what is already present in your school. In short, you were probably selected, at least to some degree, because people assumed that you could work effectively with the principal.

In the space below, indicate ways in which you might face potential conflicts between your own needs to be recognized and the needs of your principal. _____

_____

_____

_____

Indicate some of the ways in which you might work to resolve these potential conflicts between your principal and your ego. _____

_____

_____

_____

_____

SUMMARIZING THE CHAPTER

This chapter considered one of the many pieces of advice given to those who serve as assistant principals, namely not to let your personal sense of importance or need to be perceived as a great leader by others get in the way of your primary duty of assisting your principal. Regardless of whether you work for the greatest principal in the world or a person who is extremely inept or incompetent, you are where you are because you are needed to do some things that another person cannot do. It was also noted that your long-term goals and ambitions cannot be achieved if others perceive you in a negative light. Instead, being a good team member, ready to pitch in and assist, will always be your most valuable characteristic at this point in your career.

6

Assist the Principal

Roberta Shaw was happy to get the phone call from Steve Ahrends, Director of Human Resources for the Marin City Schools, who told her that she had been selected as one of the three new assistant principals who would be working in the district next year. She would join Carlos Diaz and Amos Graham to take an administrative position for the first time. Naturally, she asked Mr. Ahrends where she would be assigned, but the Director could say only that exact placement decisions would not be made for a few days. "It all depends on a few variables that we'll need to review here at the central office."

Roberta's first response to the phone call was very positive. After all, she had been working hard for the past three years toward obtaining an administrative position. But now she began to wonder when she would get her big chance. There were three openings in the district for assistants, and she assumed that all openings would be assigned to the "rookies." There were no rumors of any lateral transfers of veteran assistants. One opening was at Kleinschmidt Middle School where the principal, Martha Ortiz, had been a well-respected principal for many years. She had a reputation for being very demanding of everyone, particularly her assistants. Working with her would be tough, but Martha also had a reputation for being quite fair. Besides that, her last three assistants became principals in the district very quickly.

Juan Armendariz was the principal of the second school with an opening, Carlsbad High School. Being assigned there would be Roberta's first choice. She had known Juan for several years, and she believed that he would be willing to work with her and guide her during her time at the school. Not only that, but Carlsbad was known as one of the best high schools in the state. Being associated with the school, particularly with a helpful principal as a mentor, could be a real "career maker" for a young administrator.

The third opening was anything but a dream job. It would be to serve as the fifth assistant principal in the past four years at Pilegrove Middle School. From what Roberta had heard, there was nothing wrong with the school or the teachers. But Arnie Kilgore, the principal, had a horrible reputation among teachers and administrators in the district. For one thing, he was seen as quite arrogant, and he was known as an administrator who never listened to anyone else. He was described as a principal who "sits in his office all the time and makes what many former staff members referred to as unreasonable demands of people." At the same time, those who responded to his directions never seemed to receive any credit for actually doing the work that was assigned. He had limited interpersonal skills, and his tone of voice seemed to be a sarcastic whine that aggravated most people he met. The word was that the superintendent and many other central office administrators knew of Arnie's shortcomings, but the principal was the "fair-haired boy" of a couple of school board members. When challenged, Arnie was always quick to point out that he would probably "outlive all the other principals in the district" because he was "connected."

Roberta was dreaming of starting her career, hopefully with her friend, Juan, when the phone rang at her house. It was Mr. Ahrends who calmly said, "Roberta, you'll be at Pilegrove in the fall."

Roberta learned some important lessons through this experience. Above everything else, she recognized the truth of an old saying she had heard on many occasions from friends who became school administrators in the last few years. "Remember that when you get hired, you are hired as an employee of the district, not of a single school in particular," was something that she had heard over and over again. In her mind, she knew that when you apply for an administrative position, the district has the right to place you in a position that meets the district's needs, not yours. Whether that practice is good or not may be debatable. After all, there is some sense that an individual school's needs should define the kind of person hired as an administrator. But the fact is, school districts have many priorities that need to be served through the assignment of administrative personnel. "Perfect" matches may be desirable, but they often do not occur. In reality, if Roberta had applied for a single opening, not one of three, she would still have had no guarantee that she would be placed at the school with the apparent opening. Many things happen between the time when a position is advertised and it is filled. The district could have seen Roberta as an excellent applicant for a position needing her special talents, skills, or background. Or, there may have been a need to make other transfers of personnel that resulted in a shift of newly hired administrators. She also knew that, even if her assignment was at a "horrible school," she dared not refuse the offer. If she did, she might never be offered another administrative position in her school district. She recalled the words of a former professor who advised her, "Never apply for a position you may not really want."

Admittedly, in smaller school systems, you may not be subject to the same last-minute disappointments or uncertainties faced by the job applicants in this scenario. But the issue remains one to consider, even if you are working in a small district with one or two schools. If you are interested in applying for an assistant principalship, you must appreciate the fact that you will need to work effectively with the principal. And the fact is that whether you believe the principal is very effective or very ineffective, this is still the principal you are being selected to assist.

After not getting her first choice, Roberta now had to accept her new job with grace and a strong commitment to keep a few important ideas in mind.

KNOW YOUR JOB

Above all, remember that your single most critical duty as an assistant principal is to assist your principal. The first reaction you might have to this recommendation is that this is so obvious a statement it is not even worth noting. After all, that is what is stated in your formal job description, particularly the part about the expectation that assistant principals will "do all reasonable and job-related duties assigned by the principal in addition to those enumerated in the job description." There are, of course, many situations where a strong effort is made to ensure that an administrative team is actually formed, where no single administrator serves as the hierarchical leader. But the fact is, even with participative leadership and efforts to include all stakeholders in the decision authority in a school, the principal remains the legal chief executive of a school campus. Simply stated, the principal is your boss, and you are to do what the boss reasonably requires you to do.

It is critical that you decide early in your term as an assistant that you are to work in harmony with the principal. Among other things, that statement implies that you are to follow the direct orders of your principal. That does not necessarily mean that you must engage in "blind obedience" to the wishes of the principal at all times. In fact, one of the most important ways of providing support is not only doing what you are told to do, but also by making your principal look good and achieve success as the leader of your school. After all, if being a school leader means "doing things that improve the education of children," your focus should always be on doing what is needed to achieve that goal. You may have to learn how to live with the fact that you will need to suppress what may be a natural desire to call attention to your own talents and accomplishments. You cannot "show up" the principal. To some extent, you need to remain in the shadows. Referring back to the scenario that opened this chapter, that may be quite easy if your principal is like Martha or Juan. After all, both show evidence of having a sense of how to work with their assistant principals. If you are working with someone who is not quite capable or effective, however, you may have a very different task. The issue that you need to begin with is an assessment of your present principal's ability to serve as your mentor. Remember, though, that no one is perfect. Even the best principals have limitations, and the most limited principals will have some strengths. You can learn from anyone if you have the right attitude and you are committed to doing your job.

What are some of the strongest characteristics that you can learn from your current principal? _____

_____

_____

_____

_____

As an assistant, how can you help your principal in ways that will capitalize on these strengths to help the school? (For example, perhaps you note that your principal is extremely strong with the "big picture" related to introducing new ideas and practices to the staff. Can you enable the principal's talents to shine even brighter by taking on the task of dealing with the details that may be needed to allow good ideas to flourish even though they are not clearly addressed by the principal?) _____

_____

_____

_____

_____

_____

How can you learn to apply your principal's special skills to your work as an educational leader? _____

_____

_____

_____

_____

On the other side, what are some of the limitations of your principal? How can you serve by adding skills that you possess so that your principal's limitations may be less visible? (For example, if you are skilled at managing time, and your principal always seems to be "running late" or does not have the ability to end meetings in a timely fashion, are there any ways that you can subtly "administer" your boss's calendar and daily schedule?)

_____

_____

_____

_____

Be patient. A couple of things will likely happen if you "keep your nose down and just do your job." If you are fortunate, an extremely capable and effective principal will no doubt recognize that you have been quietly and patiently waiting in the wings. For the most part, appreciation may not be shown immediately or even particularly visibly, but a good principal will discern competence and a job well done. Remember that in the majority of cases your good principal was probably also a very good assistant principal at one time.

On the other hand, you may be assisting a person who is less than effective and capable. In fact, you may be working with the worst principal in the school district. Continue to be supportive and continue to do everything you can to make the principal look good. It may be frustrating, and it almost certainly will mean a lot of hard work, but remember at least two things. First, if you do a good job of covering for an ineffective principal, you will be doing what can be done to help your school—teachers, staff, and, most critically, students. Second, if you are able to discern that your principal is ineffective, that is probably not a classified secret that is unknown to the superintendent, other principals, central office staff, school board members, and no doubt parents and the community at large. Do you really think that, in the opening scenario, the behavior of Arnie Kilgore at Pilegrove Middle School was not apparent to most people in the district? If you do your job each day as an assistant principal, and you can make good things happen for your school and boss, a lot of people will quickly recognize that the ineffective principal has someone doing a great job; they will know who is really doing the work.

However, if you take the attitude that because you are stuck with an ineffective principal, and you do not have to work very hard, something else will likely happen. If you do not do the job that your principal ought to be doing, your school will likely begin to look quite poor to those who are reviewing its performance. Whether or not you believe it is fair, others may begin to see you as an administrator of a failing school. Your career could understandably suffer as a result of your leadership role in what seems to be a bad school. It may be an unfair case of "guilt by association," but outsiders often paint their criticisms with a rather broad brush. Remember that, in many cases, you may not always get the kudos that should follow good things happening in a school where you serve as an assistant. However, there is a good chance that you will be blamed for failures as quickly as your principal might.

What are some of the specific ways in which you can increase your personal status and appearance of competence by helping your principal succeed? _____

_____

_____

_____

_____

COMMUNICATION IS THE KEY

The most important step you need to take to work effectively with your principal is to keep channels of communication open at all times. As you work toward your goal of being supportive, your principal needs to know about you, and in turn, you need to know the vision, goals, interests, strengths, and limitations of your principal.

If you return to the scenario at the beginning of this chapter, you might put yourself in Roberta's place or in the place of one of the other two beginning assistant principals. In all probability, the principal that might be most appealing to you is Juan Armendariz, who is seen as a person people can talk with and as someone with the potential of being a really good mentor. You might also consider what it would be like to work with Martha Ortiz, the middle school principal with a reputation of being a demanding but fair principal. After all, she had a pretty decent track record of having former assistants move into principalships rather quickly. You probably would not relish the idea of working with Arnie Kilgore, the apparently very ineffective principal who stayed in his office all the time. But then, like Roberta, you probably would not have a choice. If you want to be successful and work effectively with the principal, you need to be able to communicate.

If you considered each of the three principals described in this chapter, what strategies would you need to use in establishing a pattern of open and honest communication in each case? _____

_____

_____

_____

_____

If you are now an assistant, what approaches do you need to use to work out an effective approach to communicating with your current principal? If you are now an aspiring school administrator, what approaches do you intend to adopt when you serve as an assistant principal? _____

_____

_____

_____

_____

Regardless of the specific skills of your principal or the nature of the relationship with each other, there are a few suggested activities that you may wish to consider in an effort to get to know more about your administrative colleague, while you become less of a stranger.

1. *Talk about your platforms.* Chapter 2 described the importance of taking the time to reflect on the core values that you have as an educator and then writing down a few key reflections on these values. This is a

highly recommended activity for newly hired school administrators, and it is also a good practice for even the most senior and experienced principal. Even if these statements of beliefs and values are not formally written down, every educator has thought about virtually each one of the items (and many others) that was listed earlier in this book. You may wish to suggest that, at the beginning of your first year with the principal, you spend some time talking about ways in which the two of you have some similar perspectives on a variety of issues. Discovering where actual or potential differences may exist between a principal and an assistant is a valuable activity. This may be done through a formal sharing of written platforms, or simply by having one or more brief conversations that focus on issues normally included in a platform statement.

It becomes considerably easier to support and work with someone who shares some of your views about educational issues. Even if you and the principal are at polar opposites on some or even most things, however, it is better to understand these differences early in the school year.

2. *Share duties together.* In schools where there is only one assistant to work with the principal, it may be tempting to split all duty assignments to maximize coverage by two separate administrators. This may be a wise and practical approach to distributing most duty assignments such as after school sports coverage, bus duty, or many other instances when only one administrator at a time may be needed. On occasion, however, the principal and assistant may want to work deliberately together as a team. Two really good things happen by doing this, even if it is not done all the time. First, seeing the two administrators together at some events and in different settings during the school day sends a message to both staff and students that there is a leadership *team* at work in their school. This may be extremely critical in cases where the principal has not had a history of being visible around the school. This suggestion does not mean that you and the principal should spend all of your time together to present a visible "united front," just that it can be important nonverbal communication.

A second result of sharing duty with your principal is that it provides a lot of opportunities when the two of you can have extended time for talking about issues that need to be considered by the administrative team. Working together at a few basketball games, track meets, or band concerts allows you not only to provide visible coverage of after-school events, but it allows the principal and you to talk about a variety of issues that you may not be able to touch on during a typical, busy day. As one experienced principal known as an outstanding mentor to beginning administrators in his district observed, "I've done a lot of serious career counseling while standing on the sidelines of football games, talking with my assistants."

In some schools, principals and assistants deliberately schedule themselves for supervision in the cafeteria. First, this enables teachers to get a bit of needed time away from the students during the day. After all, teacher expertise is not needed to observe kids in a cafeteria. Second, although administrative credentials are not required to watch over lunch rooms, this can be a valuable time for engaging in conversation and also for getting to know the students a bit better. After all, one of the things that you no doubt will discover as a school administrator is that you do not have regular access to average students as often as you did when you were a teacher. By walking around the cafeteria each day, you have instant access to hundreds of the people your job was created to serve in the first place.

3. *Schedule regular meetings.* Many campus administrators establish a specific time at least once each week when they get together to talk and think about important issues facing the campus. This time can also be used to decide a duty roster for activities during the week, how to respond to some new district initiatives, set timelines, and so forth. Normally, these meetings might be first thing on Monday mornings, or even late on Friday afternoons.

4. *Have a meal together.* If you are already an assistant principal, you have no doubt discovered that having a meal in your school is often a luxury. On many days, an apple or a candy bar and a cup of coffee must suffice for lunch. Another way that you and the principal can spend some time getting to understand each other is by occasionally finding time to go to the cafeteria or even to sneak out of the building for a fast lunch break. Simply being away from the crowds at school can offer important opportunities for communication.

DEVELOPING AN ACTION PLAN

Describe some of the ways in which you plan to support your principal and to learn as a result of your action. If you are not yet serving as an assistant, what are some of the ways that you anticipate being able to support your principal? _____

_____

_____

_____

_____

Indicate strategies you intend to follow in establishing regular opportunities for communicating with your building principal throughout the year. If you are already an assistant, how do you now communicate regularly with your administrative colleagues? _____

_____

_____

_____

_____

As is true with all open-ended questions such as those listed above, the ultimate value of thinking about answers is not found simply in your immediate answers. Make certain to return to your reflective statements from time to time during your first year or two as an administrator. If you are not yet serving as an administrator, review your comments with critical friends and mentors who are assisting you in your preparation and formation as a school leader. And above all, be willing to add to or modify any or all of your best intentions as you continue with your career.

SUMMARIZING THE CHAPTER

This chapter considered another critical point to remember as an assistant principal. Whether you are working with a very effective principal or with one who is not necessarily a strong leader, you owe allegiance to your principal. That does not necessarily mean absolute, blind obedience at all times. It does, however, mean that you are committed to helping your principal become as successful as possible. To do less than that would be contrary to a critical duty that you and all educational leaders must recognize: that it is your job to ensure that your school becomes as effective as possible in addressing the needs of your students. Help your principal to help the children.

7

Reflect Before Speaking or Acting

What was supposed to be the fulfillment of a professional dream was becoming more like a nightmare. Jamie Pierson had been an assistant principal for nearly half a year, and she was already asking people around the district to let her know if there were any teaching positions opening for third or fourth grade next year. She had had about enough of the world of "school leadership," and she wanted to get back to where she really felt as if she were doing something with her life that benefited students.

Jamie's discontent began shortly after she received word that she had interviewed very well for a position as an assistant principal in her district, the Bridgeport Hills Local Schools. There were four positions open last summer as a result of the retirement of experienced administrators in three elementary schools and one middle school. Her immediate reaction to hearing that she would be recommended as an assistant was one of great happiness. She had been an elementary teacher for 11 years, and she felt that it was time in her professional life for some new challenges. Her joy turned to other emotions when she learned that her assignment would be at Lincoln Park Elementary, a school not even identified as one with an administrative opening when she had first applied. That was a good thing, because Jamie (and probably most others who applied) would have thought twice before taking the chance of landing a first administrative job at Lincoln Park.

On the surface, Lincoln Park did not appear to be a bad school. After all, it was located in a stylish, upper–middle-income neighborhood on the north side of the city. It was an older building on a tree-lined street near a large private university. The school community had gone through several major changes during the past 25 years or so. For a long time, the neighborhood was a solid working class community where children came from very stable homes. Then, the community began to change to include an increasing number of minority families, many of whom had just recently migrated to the United States from Central or South America. With its most recent transformation, the neighborhood was becoming "gentrified" by attracting a large number of upper–middle-class families back from the suburbs. It was a place where people could be close to their downtown offices, rely on public transportation, and find interesting ethnic stores and restaurants. The area had gone through yet another change, and Lincoln Park Elementary had changed too. Now, the majority of the students were from single-parent homes. In addition, there were great expectations that the teachers at the school would be preparing children to succeed in college in the future, which had not been the primary concern of most parents in the past.

Changes in the community over the years did not make the school unappealing as a place for assistant principals to work. The main problem seemed to be the majority of teachers and the principal, Dr. Fred Franklin, who had been together for several years at Lincoln Park and had experienced the different kinds of communities surrounding the school. During this time, scores on the statewide achievement test remained stable. The school, however, was slowly getting a reputation as a kind of short-term assignment for assistant principals. There had been four in the past five years; one year had featured two assistants. Jamie heard through many colleagues in the district that the culprit was Dr. Franklin and what were described as his unreasonable demands and even less reasonable expectations. People seemed to get out of there as soon as possible, either to other schools in the district or through placements in surrounding communities.

Jamie was concerned about the assignment, but she made up her mind to do her best, regardless of the challenges that she faced. She had worked much too hard getting ready for this opportunity. She started the year with good intentions and a very positive attitude, but soon Dr. Franklin's reputation began to be proven accurate. What's more, his "inner circle" of teachers seemed to be a part of the problem that Jamie was now beginning to face.

Jamie soon began to understand a reality of any administrative position: It is a lonely job. Jamie needed to talk, to vent, to express her frustrations to someone, but she knew that she had to be quite careful in selecting her confidantes. Fortunately, she knew two teachers at Lincoln Park quite well from her undergraduate days at local Northern and Western University. In fact, the three students spent hours imagining both good and bad scenarios that they would face when they got jobs "in the real world." So far, the experiences Jamie was having bordered on "beyond the bad" scenarios. She needed to get together and talk with her old college friends.

The three friends gathered on a Saturday at a nice, quiet inn located in a suburb several miles from Lincoln Park. Although she felt a bit melodramatic in doing so, Jamie was careful to scope out the restaurant as soon as they entered, looking for any familiar faces from her school. After a few minutes, the former classmates began to talk shop and Jamie nearly exploded with the opportunity to begin her litany of concerns since arriving at the school. Anne Sirois, a third-grade teacher for the past six years at Lincoln Park, quickly agreed and added her own examples of the frustrations associated with working with Dr. Franklin. Penny Thomas, the other teacher in the group, sat silently during the conversation and added only a few vague comments and an occasional smile or frown. Jamie assumed that Penny stayed away from the conversation because she was relatively new not only to Lincoln Park, but to the school district. The luncheon turned into a conversation lasting several hours. Finally, when the group parted, Jamie felt enormously relieved at having been able to gripe, gossip, and finally begin to gain what she believed to be some needed perspective. Everything would be better on Monday morning.

When Jamie arrived at school to start the next week, she sensed some inordinate coolness on the part of the head secretary and two or three teachers. She thought nothing of it other than it was the usual "Monday morning blues" that afflicted many workers in all organizations. But she froze in her tracks when Dr. Franklin walked past her and mentioned that he hoped she had had a good weekend but she needed to stop by his office as soon as morning announcements were finished. He had "some very distressing matters to discuss with her."

Jamie first put the comment aside in her mind, but the next hour or so was an agonizing experience as she suddenly began to review the luncheon on Saturday. Had she made a horrible error?

Does the ending of this scenario immediately tell you that Jamie is in "big trouble" with the principal because she met with her friends on Saturday? Was Penny a traitor who could never be trusted again? Was Jamie's job in trouble? What would happen to her career? Would she ever become a principal? Although it may sound a bit like the opening to a soap opera, all of these are reasonable questions for a person to review under these circumstances. But the fact is, at this moment, the "distressing matter" that the principal wants to discuss may have nothing at all to do with Jamie. Guilt often seizes control of people in similar settings.

The purpose of this chapter is not to second-guess Jamie or decide why she may or may not be in trouble with her principal. Instead, the point here is to describe yet another important thing to keep in mind when you take on an administrative post for the first time. Although it is not a particularly eloquent sentiment, it is a critical, practical tip that you need to learn early in your career. Simply stated, know when to talk, but more important, learn when to keep quiet and reflect on issues once you become an assistant principal.

WHY?

Whether you are blessed by working with a great principal or you work with someone less capable, remember that you owe your colleague discretion and loyalty. A big part of these qualities is learning not to badmouth your principal, gossip, leak information to others, or, above all, disagree publicly with your principal. As a school administrator, you will have access to many things that must be kept confidential, not only by law, but also because certain information may have a negative impact on people with whom you work. By the same token, you will make the job of your principal much more difficult by talking behind his or her back. It will be a temptation, if you are drawn into conversations with teachers, other administrators, parents, or community members, to say things that might be taken as critical of the principal's work. There is an old saying that if others hear you speaking ill of someone, they will begin to wonder if you speak ill of them in their absence. It is a saying worth thinking about.

The suggestion that schools are often places where gossip about the work of others is commonplace may or may not shock you. If you agree with this observation, provide some examples from your experience that illustrate the kinds of things that educators say about their colleagues (other teachers, administrators, counselors, or others). _____

_____

_____

_____

_____

In cases where talk by educators has been critical of colleagues, what have been some of the negative effects of this type of activity on the person being criticized? What about the impact on those who have been critics?

_____

_____

_____

_____

Return to the opening scenario of this chapter. What mistakes did Jamie make by sharing her concerns with her teacher friends? What are the likely negative consequences for Jamie because of her comments? _____

_____

_____

_____

_____

WHY NOT?

There are, of course, certain times when it may be necessary to disagree with something done (or not done) by your principal. In these cases it is not only acceptable but also your professional duty to be candid with your colleague. You need to express your concerns. You might be able to have an opportunity to change a practice, policy, or decision. But, depending on the situation, you might also learn a few things about effective practice, as well. Despite what you see on the surface, there are likely to be reasons guiding a certain decision. Experienced principals may often do things that at first appear to be wrong, not smart, foolish, unwise, or even downright dumb. Depending on the situation, you might also learn a few things about effective administrative practice. Not assuming the worst when you see a principal doing something that you might not do is a good opportunity to learn. You might ask a simple question, such as, "Why did you do what you did?" Don't judge. Learn. Your question may also have another positive, unintended consequence. Your principal may take it as an opportunity to reflect on his or her behavior. Often, experienced administrators get into an understandable habit of doing things the same way, over and over, in the belief that "it always works." Having an outsider ask "Why?" may cause some needed personal reassessment.

Have you had any experiences so far where you have unexpectedly learned something about administering a school by seeing your principal do something that you did not agree with at first? What did you learn? _____

_____

_____

_____

_____

The point of all of this is that disagreeing with your principal is acceptable. Rash and harsh public criticism is not.

TIPS FOR EFFECTIVE DISAGREEMENT

On those occasions when it is necessary to communicate your disagreement with the principal, here are some tips you may wish to consider.

Be Direct

First, if you disagree with something, say it directly to the principal, not to half the teachers in the school. Do not even selectively talk to "confidantes," as our beginning assistant principal in the opening case study did. This is important for at least two reasons. In the first case, you owe candor and directness to your principal. Running a school or assisting the person in charge of a school is not an easy responsibility. It is simply too important a job to create an environment where adults cannot communicate concerns to one another. It may be quite difficult for you to be direct, and you might be too intimidated to talk to the boss about some reservations you have. Simply stated, you have to grow professionally beyond such concerns. The second reason for not talking to others about your concerns is that you may quickly discover that some of your long-standing "friends" are less concerned about you than you had hoped. Jamie was naïve to assume that people with whom she had worked as a teacher were likely to have the same feelings of allegiance to her now that she was in a position of authority and control as an administrator.

What are some other reasons for developing the ability to confront your principal (or anyone else) about your honest disagreements regarding matters of professional practice? Even if you are not currently an assistant, you have probably had disagreements with colleagues over the years. How did you handle these disagreements? _____

_____

_____

_____

_____

Be Discreet

Another tip for how you may convey disagreement to your principal is always say what you have to say behind closed doors. Perhaps the best analogy here might be that disagreements between colleagues, as between spouses, should never be "in front of the kids." To do so can easily encourage those who seek opportunities for dissension to divide and conquer. No one is asking you to park your brain on the curb outside your school each day. You do not need to become a fawning "Yes" person who hovers around the principal, deferring to every wish as if it were a golden command. However, when you disagree with something that your boss says or does, you have a professional responsibility to decide if it is of such consequence that you must bring it up. If you do, remain discreet and courteous by discussing it in private.

Always remember that the business of operating a school must be guided primarily by engaging in activities that are directly related to the learning needs of students. Frequent disagreement between members of the management or leadership team causes turmoil in a school. It will disrupt faculty morale, and it is anything but a good situation for anyone. For the students in a school in which such situations exist, it is truly like having constant bickering between parents in an unhappy home.

If you were to spend time with your principal (in a private session behind closed doors) and discuss some of the ways in which you might disagree with some of the things requested of you or said to you, what might they be? If you are not currently an assistant principal, how do you plan to deal with the need to provide honest feedback to your colleague? _____

_____

_____

_____

_____

SUMMARIZING THE CHAPTER

This chapter provided another important way in which you may be able to ensure a more successful professional experience as an assistant principal. Specifically, it noted that many assistant principals may have career problems because they have not learned that their job is to do, not to talk. Moreover, the kind of talking that will be most detrimental to anyone's professional well-being consists of grumbling, griping, and gossiping. If you remember the points made in previous chapters about the need to cool your ego and support the principal, you will no doubt appreciate the value of hearing that your job is not to instruct your boss. While you may have many good ideas to share, and you may also be faced with the reality of working with someone with whom you frequently disagree, remember that there is always an appropriate time and place to share your concerns. Above all, that time and place is never behind the principal's back.

In your life as a school administrator, conflict will always be part of your daily reality. Conflict must be addressed openly and honestly, however, not used as a kind of weapon to control others. While you are an assistant principal, you will rarely, if ever, be on the winning side of any contest that pits you against the principal. If you wish to be critical, be direct and discreet. If you are not able to follow that simple suggestion, follow the title of this chapter.

8

Listen, Listen . . . Then Listen Some More

"So I told her that I had never heard of someone doing that with the student council before. In fact, at the last school where I taught, in another school district, the principal always made it a point to provide the students with their own space and let them go off on their own to decide their business. After all, how else are the kids going to learn?"

With that closing statement, Letty Salas was out of the teachers' lounge and headed off for afternoon supervision of the attendance procedures in the main office. The three teachers in the lounge just smiled at her while she was on her soapbox making what seemed to be a daily speech about how she could do a better job of running Carol Canyon High School than the present principal, Sarah Clifton. Sarah had been the principal of Carol Canyon, a large high school enrolling nearly 3,000 students, for more than nine years. It was a school that had seen a great deal of change and progress over the years. When Sarah came on board there had been a great deal of racial strife in the school, gang activity, and almost daily "sweeps" for drugs carried out by the city police department and their canine units. It was a school with extremely low scores on the statewide achievement test each year. Since Sarah's arrival, things had improved greatly. Although it was far from a "perfect" school, it had gone well beyond its former image in the community. There was still a lot to do. All of this made the teachers in the lounge begin to reflect on their new assistant principal and her rather outspoken approach to working at the school.

Letty Salas was one of five assistant principals in the school. The others had several years of administrative experience at either Carol Canyon or other large high schools in the district. Letty was a bit of an unknown quantity, though. She had a great reputation as a special education teacher at Clear Aire Middle School, the largest intermediate school in the neighboring Towering Falls Local School District. She also did a great job of interviewing when she came to the school as a finalist candidate last spring. But there were reservations expressed by many because she was truly a rookie who had never worked in a high school, let alone one as large and complex as Carol Canyon. When Sarah made her final decision, however, it was based on several factors that others had not considered. For one thing, Letty was bilingual (English and Spanish), and no other member of the administrative team had this skill. Carol Canyon was increasingly becoming a majority Latino school, and having someone able to speak fluently with parents, students, and community members was a plus. Second, Letty had a very strong background in special education, an area in which the school had been without an administrative representative for many years. A recent evaluation by the state department of education had noted this as a deficiency in the school.

Letty got off to a good start. She was affable, outgoing, and her linguistic and teaching expertise soon became respected by teachers, staff, and the other administrators. But there was one thing that also became quickly recognized about the new assistant principal. She seemed to have an opinion about everything, and she expressed her views constantly. One of the secretaries in the school's main office once made the remark that she wondered "if Ms. Salas ever had a moment to breathe—she seemed to be talking all the time."

Actually, Letty's talking was not the real problem. She did not seem to know how to converse. Her soliloquy in the teacher's lounge about "how the principal needed to let the students make their own decisions" was an example of typical behavior that was quickly annoying many. Letty's statements were often preceded by references to "what my last principal did" or "what we did in my old school district." It seemed to matter very little what was said prior to Letty's statements. She was not in the habit of listening before she began to explain to everyone around her what she knew about one topic or another. It was getting to the point where the other assistant principals were actually beginning to avoid bringing any issue of concern to Letty. Perhaps most distressing was the fact that Sarah Clifton, the principal, was also spending no time with her most recently hired assistant.

To put it bluntly, Letty Salas is in big trouble as a rookie assistant principal. Like most administrative newcomers, she is going through a period of review by her colleagues, who are waiting to see what the "new person" is able to do and how she is going to deal with the responsibilities and duties of an assistant principal. In addition, there is some evidence that Letty was not coming in with the strongest background as a candidate. She clearly had a lot to learn because she had no prior administrative experience, and her professional career did not include any time spent in a high school. Finally, this was not simply "any" high school. As the new assistant no doubt would have known prior to applying for the position, this school had a great many past problems, and there would still be many challenges for anyone—experienced or not. It would be a good idea for anyone coming to the school to get a handle on what was happening there. No one would expect the new person to jump in immediately and solve all the problems faced by the school, so the first few months or even first year could be classified as a time for learning a lot.

Unfortunately, this newly appointed assistant principal did not seem to realize that her job was to be a learner, not a fount of information to all who could hear her. She had been hired to join an administrative team, not serve as the star in the center of a stage. With her limited experience, placement as an assistant principal in a large comprehensive high school was an opportunity for Letty to grow. At present, however, that opportunity for growth was seemingly quite limited.

LISTEN BEFORE DECIDING

As described in past chapters, the great advantage of adopting a stance in which you reflect before talking and cool your ego is that you are likely to learn a lot of things very quickly. You can do this through a very simple learning technique that you have no doubt shared with hundreds of students enrolled in your classes over the years. That technique is simply to listen and absorb.

One of the realities of being an assistant principal in your first formal job in school administration is that people likely realize that you do not have a great deal of prior experience as a manager. Although you may get into situations in which you feel as if you must act and take a strong stance because, after all, you are now an administrator, keep in mind the old saying that, at times, the best decisions are often those that are not made—at least not immediately.

A constant temptation for those who are new to administration is to attempt to demonstrate their skills and insights by taking immediate, decisive action on everything that comes across their desk. It's almost as if an unwritten set of instructions exists that says, "You are weak if you put off any decision." It may be true that there are those in your school who will push you for a quick answer on virtually every issue. And, in fact, most of those people will be your strongest allies—if you consistently decide issues according to their preferences. However, you may also quickly learn another remarkable fact of life in the world of school administration: "Good" administrators often become "bad" administrators overnight based on the strength of making only one contrary decision!

Have you had any examples of losing supporters based on only one or a few decisions that you made that were contrary to the wishes of former "followers"? If so, describe the situation and then indicate whether you were surprised by this outcome. _____

_____

_____

_____

_____

There is no effort here to suggest that you should avoid making any decisions just because you are new or because you are an assistant principal. As you can probably understand even before becoming an administrator, there are too many schools that frequently suffer from a type of organizational paralysis that comes about because of decision avoidance by superintendents, school board members, principals, or others. But absolute, unyielding, and often rash decisions are equally unproductive. Two things are useful to remember to help you decide the proper balance between paralysis and authoritarianism.

First, as an assistant principal, you have not only the opportunity but also the duty to defer many of your most challenging decisions to a higher authority, namely your principal. This statement should not make you feel as if you are turning and running away from making a decision, or that you are not doing your job because you are passing a tough job along to the boss. Rather, it is always important that, as the chief administrator of a school, the principal is legally and ethically responsible for all that occurs within the school. Referring a really tough decision to the principal is not a mark of your weakness. Rather, it is a sign that you understand the ways in which a school must function.

Can you provide any examples of decisions that you made that probably should have been referred to the principal? How about decisions that you forwarded to the principal, but you should probably have handled on your own? If you are not yet an assistant principal, what can you imagine to be examples of these types of decisions? _____

_____

_____

_____

_____

This leads to a second recommendation for learning effective decision making by listening. One of the reasons your principal has that job is usually because of greater experience as an administrator. That probably means that even when you do not necessarily agree with some stances taken by your boss, it is likely that they have a foundation in past practice. The only way that you are likely to achieve that same degree of experience is by remaining open to the thoughts of others and listening, observing, and asking questions so that you can listen some more. The key here is to adopt an attitude of willingness to learn by absorbing as much as possible.

List three to five aspects of school administration that you have learned since taking your position by simply listening to what your principal has said or by observing what your principal has done. Again, if you are not yet in that role, think of some parallel situations where you learned a lot by simply listening. _____

_____

_____

_____

_____

Of course, it is possible to learn positive administrative practice even when you listen to or observe less-than-effective ideas or actions by a poor role model. The key, of course, is to keep any comments about the limitations of your boss to yourself, perhaps vowing never to do what you have seen or heard when you become a principal on your own.

CAN YOU LISTEN TOO MUCH?

In a word, the answer is "No." Whether you are working alongside a brilliant "principal of the year" candidate or a person who might be described as hopelessly incompetent (in your eyes, at least), you have a lot to learn. You may find yourself looking forward to some quality time when you can simply sit back and listen to and watch a very gifted leader handle a problem. Perhaps a really demanding parent who has been a thorn in your side is suddenly calmed because of the way in which your principal deals with a concern. Or a scheduling conflict that you thought was impossible to reconcile is suddenly addressed by the principal's intervention. In other cases, you may find that you are losing patience with yet another war story describing "how we used to do it back when this was a real junior high school, not a middle school." Or you may hear a solution to a complex problem that is simplistic, ignoring the central problem that is brought to the principal. In either case, listen and learn.

The idea of listening as much as possible needs to be tempered a bit by your need to learn as you absorb what others do. There is no suggestion that you should never question the reasons and assumptions made by your principal. In fact, asking the question, "Why did you take such and such a stance?" from time to time may be helpful to both you and the principal, as noted in the previous chapter. In any case, it is a far better approach than the one followed by Letty in our opening scenario as she seemed bound and determined to convince the principal that she had the answers that were needed by the student council.

List some of the ways in which you have already learned more about being an effective leader by listening and absorbing from more experienced colleagues with whom you now work. _____

_____

_____

_____

_____

A FEW TIPS

Simply learning that it is often far better to listen than not may be helpful, but the question that might arise here is "How?" Besides committing yourself to silence and listening a lot, there are a few ideas that you may wish to consider.

First, ask your principal if it is possible to engage in periodic shadowing of his or her work as a principal. Select a time when you are able to watch and follow your colleague, not as an evaluator, but only as a person who wants to watch and listen and learn. This type of shadowing process need not represent a massive time commitment for either you or the principal. It is possible to learn much through silent observation of an active principal for an hour or so. And it does not have to be an "every day" or "every week" activity. All that is suggested here is that, on occasion, you make an arrangement to follow your principal during a normal, routine hour of activity, whether in the office or walking around the school. It does not matter if you do this during a major event or simply day-in and day-out work. You are there to watch and learn. The most important thing to remember is that you are not there to volunteer comments or solutions. Unless invited, just watch and listen. Then talk with the principal after the observation has concluded.

If you cannot organize any formal observation time, follow a recommendation made in an earlier chapter and see if you can do common duty with the principal. Supervising cafeterias is a particularly good opportunity. Informal conversations that take place while walking around a lunchroom can be a gold mine of information. Or standing around watching the bleachers at a football game or a basketball game can give you access to the principal in ways that are not typically available during a busy school day.

If your principal has not already suggested it, try to establish a regular ten- to fifteen-minute period near the beginning of each week when you and the principal can talk through the activities for the next few days. Again, be aware that the purpose is for you to listen and observe, not dictate your needs to the principal.

Are there any other ways in which you might be able to organize some time during the day or week in which you can have access to your principal as a source of information? _____

_____

_____

_____

_____

SUMMARIZING THE CHAPTER

This chapter opened with the story of a beginning assistant principal who clearly has yet to recognize that she is in a great place to learn a lot about school leadership. She is working in a challenging school with an experienced principal, but she has yet to appreciate that she was not hired for her overall expertise as an administrator. She could learn a great deal, but first she has to learn how to listen.

The chapter also included a number of suggestions for ways in which you might be able to increase your learning as an assistant principal. In order to do this, however, it is critical to observe and listen. Always keep in mind that, regardless of whether you see your service as an assistant as a "first step" in an administrative career that will lead you to the principalship or a central office role or if you are quite content to remain as an assistant principal, you have a clear goal: becoming the best educational leader that you can become. One way to make that goal a reality is to learn from your colleagues. Listening is an important beginning in that learning process.

9

Ask to Do More

"**M**r. Pilowski is exactly the kind of person we need for this job!" said Steve Freeman, a math teacher. That statement was echoed by several of the teachers at Hopkins Middle School. Since the retirement last December of Sam Hawkins, former coach and assistant principal for many years, the school of more than 1,500 students had been operating with only two administrators. That wasn't what concerned many staff, however. Both the principal, Dr. Helen O'Malley, and the remaining assistant, Jane Pierson, were acknowledged to be fine educators who cared about the students, school, and staff. However, both individuals spent most of their time on instruction and curriculum. Since Sam's retirement, no one was devoted to student discipline in quite the same way, and the teachers were getting tired of taking care of all the problems.

Michael Pilowski was energetic and known around the district as one of the really "bright young stars" headed into school administration. He had been a highly regarded math teacher at two middle schools, and he had been an assistant football coach for the past five years at one of the district's three high schools. Since he was physically a very big person, he was also known as one of the teachers who could "control the kids" pretty well.

When Michael decided to begin working on his master's degree and administrative certification, he knew that he would probably begin his administrative career as an assistant principal somewhere in the district, and he also knew that, largely because of his reputation, he would have his share of work as a disciplinarian. Even so, he really looked forward to the day when he could get involved with instructional leadership. To attain that responsibility, he wanted to move toward becoming an effective principal of a school of his own in the near future.

As the year began, Mr. Pilowski was indeed becoming just what the teachers wanted. He did a great job of handling the discipline for the entire school. He quickly became known as a no-nonsense assistant principal who dealt fairly but quickly and decisively with student behavior problems. Both the principal and the other assistant principal were extremely pleased to see that their new colleague was capable of relieving them of a responsibility that neither one relished. Michael Pilowski was able to take on the role of disciplinarian so well that the other administrators could really devote their time to instruction, curriculum, and staff development. This was the start of a really outstanding school year!

Toward the middle of the second half of the year, Michael began to become increasingly concerned about his career choice. By all accounts, he was doing a super job as a beginning administrator. Everyone liked him. Teachers knew he could make their lives better by establishing a strong sense of order in the school. The administrative team was happy. Parents knew they could count on Mr. Pilowski to ensure that the school was a safe and secure place for their children. In addition, the students—even those who had spent a lot of time in Michael's office—all respected Coach Pilowski as a fair person who always let them know where they stood. In fact, the only person who was becoming less satisfied with his work was Michael himself.

Michael sat in his office late one Friday looking at a stack of discipline referrals that he knew he would have to handle next week, and he was quite unhappy. How in the world would he ever become a principal at this rate?

A common problem for those who serve as assistant principals is that they often get typecast in their roles. If you are like Michael Pilowski and become either formally or informally designated the "Assistant Principal for Discipline and Attendance," and you do a great job, you may have a problem. Forever after, you may have to live with a well-deserved reputation as an outstanding disciplinarian. That is certainly not a negative statement. On the other hand, if your long-term goal is eventually to move into a principalship of your own, being locked in as a disciplinarian—and little else—is likely to prevent others from seeing all of the other things that you are capable of doing in the school. Providing fair and effective student discipline is, of course, very important, but a good principal (and good principal candidates) needs to do much more. Financial management and budget oversight, staff development, community relations, instructional improvement, and so many other responsibilities make up the life of the modern principal. If school districts do not perceive that you have the skills and experience needed to help you lead in these other areas of school administration, you may be an assistant principal for quite some time.

While the emphasis in the examples presented here is on the tendency for beginning assistant principals to be assigned to student discipline as a primary duty, it is also possible that you may become typecast in other administrative responsibilities. For example, people also assume the role of "Assistant Principal for Curriculum," with virtually no duties involving discipline, physical plant management, budgeting, or other managerial work. While this may sound like an appealing opportunity for someone whose eventual goal is to be the instructional leader of a school as its principal, remember that principals need to know about the managerial aspects of administration as well as curriculum and instruction.

As an assistant principal, have you been assigned a narrow set of responsibilities so far? What are they? _____

_____

_____

_____

_____

BUILDING YOUR PROFILE AS A LEADER

The trick to avoiding the trap of becoming cast solely as the "disciplinarian," or the "person who really knows a lot about attendance," or any of several other descriptors that might haunt you in your future career is to begin as soon as possible to build a personal professional profile that points out your well-rounded abilities. It is absolutely essential, therefore, that you work to develop skills and expertise in as many areas of campus management as you can while you serve as an assistant principal. If you are the only assistant principal in a school, it may be somewhat easier to gain experience in a fairly wide range of areas of service. On the other hand, if you are part of a larger team of assistant principals and your colleagues have already been assigned specific areas of coverage (curriculum, student activities, community relations, and so on), broadening your portfolio becomes much more complex. Remember that it is likely that some, if not all, of your colleagues have become quite comfortable in the areas in which they now work. Not everyone necessarily wants to diversify in the way that you might. If you are aiming for a principalship, you will need to increase your personal awareness of issues and concerns encountered in many different functional areas of operating a school.

The question you no doubt have is how you can guide the development of your skills in multiple areas of school management. The first logical step for you to take is to have a frank conversation with your principal about your goals and career objectives. Even though you have essentially been hired to do the job of assisting your principal, it is not likely to surprise your colleague that you have ambitions. Some day you may want to lead your own school. At the beginning of your time at your present school, it is worth the effort to explain to your principal what may be quite obvious: You need to gain insights into many different areas of school management and leadership. You may have several years of successful experience as a teacher during which you learned quite a bit about many aspects of school life. You also may have completed a very good program at a university in preparation for an administrative position, but there is never going to be any learning experience as potentially rich as the one you will go through as an assistant principal. It is, in many ways, the ultimate "administrative internship." To make it effective, you need the help and understanding of your principal.

WHERE DO YOU BEGIN?

There is, of course, more to do than simply sitting down with your principal and explaining that you also want to be a principal some day and then hope for guidance. Seeking assistance requires that you do some homework before you open the conversation. Earlier chapters in this book have included information that you may wish to use in conferencing with your principal.

Share Your Platform

Chapter 2 presented the importance of reflecting on personal values and beliefs as a foundation for effective leadership. It was strongly suggested that an important activity for you and every other educational leader involved the preparation of an educational platform.

One of the activities that you may wish to do as a beginning assistant principal is to share at least some of the major planks of your platform with your principal. Of course, whether you feel comfortable doing so depends on your personal assessment of your principal's willingness to engage in this type of conversation. You may or may not feel comfortable in opening yourself up to your colleague in this way. If you do, it can be a very effective beginning to an ongoing relationship when you express such things as your personal views of what constitutes successful student achievement, or the nature of effective community involvement in a school.

No one is suggesting that you present a comprehensive written statement of your platform to the principal. You may, however, wish to identify three or four key aspects of your professional educational belief system that would help a colleague learn more about you. _____

_____

_____

_____

_____

Consider Your Leadership Qualities

Another area that you may wish to review as a prelude to your discussion with a principal who will assist you in pursuing long-term goals is your personal assessment of leadership attributes and personalized views regarding the outcomes of effective leadership that you bring to the job as a new assistant principal. This information was reviewed in Chapter 3. You were asked to consider a number of different frameworks that identify the knowledge, skills, and qualities of effective leaders in schools and other organizations. Review the perspectives of Covey, the Association for Supervision and Curriculum Development, or the National Association of Secondary School Principals. Consider the self-assessment that you completed. Also, think about your ideal vision of a school where effective leadership has been practiced.

As you get ready to have a conference with your principal about the skills that you would like to develop as an educational leader, you may wish to identify in your own mind the areas where you believe you have specific strengths. (Depending on the relationship you have with your principal, you may wish to share the responses that you provided to the questions posed in Chapter 3.) _____

_____

_____

_____

_____

At the same time, you may also wish to identify those leadership skills identified in the literature but that are areas where you need further development: _____

_____

_____

_____

_____

Management Skills

The majority of your work as a beginning assistant principal will likely be directed toward carrying out many assigned management duties. Review Chapter 4 to identify some of the skills that you may need to implement some of the tasks that are noted as periodic responsibilities that you are going to have throughout the year. In your review, make note of any specific activities that you are likely to do as assigned duties that are included in the job description that you have been provided for this year. Now, look at the items that are not part of your regular assignment.

Of the tasks that you have not been assigned to carry out this year, what items do you first want to learn more about? _____

_____

_____

_____

_____

In discussing your plans and goals with your principal, what activities might be added to your current duties so you can begin to learn more about all the managerial duties faced by a principal? _____

_____

_____

_____

_____

VOLUNTEERING TO DO MORE

A long-standing motto of many in the military (as well as in most other walks of life) is, "Don't volunteer." Conventional wisdom suggests that if you want to survive, it is best not to tempt fate by going beyond your normal responsibilities. This advice might make a great deal of sense if a commanding officer is looking for someone to take on a particularly dangerous mission in combat, but it can be a potentially limiting factor in your career as a school leader.

Again, conventional wisdom might suggest that it is wise practice as a beginning assistant principal to do exactly what is required of you— certainly nothing less, but also nothing more. After all, you are not getting paid to do extra work, are you? Furthermore, school administrators do not get paid overtime. So why go out of your way?

The answer to the last question may simply be that you will likely always be an assistant principal (whether you want to or not) if you do not increase your value to schools. That might be an acceptable reality. Quite possibly, by being an assistant, you may have attained the highest level you wish to reach in your career. You may in fact really like to work with student discipline, or building maintenance, or many of the other tasks that might be assigned to you right now. The value in doing something that is limited, but doing it well, is that you are much less likely to fail. After all, the more duties you are assigned, the more probable it is that you will not succeed at some tasks. What's more, your level of accountability is much lower as an assistant principal. A principal truly sits in a "hot seat" by assuming the ultimate responsibility for all that occurs in a school. By being second in command for your entire career, you can always point to "the boss" as the reason for anything that goes wrong. Of course, taking that attitude will also ensure that you will never get full credit for what goes right, but at least your "neck is not on the chopping block."

On the other hand, you may have as a serious career and personal goal the opportunity to find your own hot seat some day and be a principal or even a superintendent. If that is the case, you cannot afford to become known as "a terrific disciplinarian, but someone who has no experience with budgeting or curriculum development or the many other things that a principal needs to know." What that means is that you need to learn about budgeting, curriculum development, and many other areas. The only way to do that is to go beyond your normally assigned duties and volunteer for extra work. Ask your principal if you can observe when it comes to reviewing and preparing the school's budget. Volunteer to work with teachers on curriculum projects. Learn how to schedule. If you are in a school with multiple assistant principals, ask for tips concerning effective ways to do the duties they do, too. If possible, you can ask your principal if you can be assigned new duties in the future.

Talking to your principal and other colleagues about their finding ways to involve you in different administrative responsibilities may not always be possible. After all, it may be that you are the only assistant principal in the school, and if the principal prefers to do certain things (e.g., curriculum and staff development), it is unlikely that you will be able to diversify in your present school. If that is the case, you may need to think about seeking a transfer to a different assignment. Many might question the wisdom of this advice. Traditionally, there has been a view that lateral transfers are negative: Don't go somewhere else to do the same job. In this case, however, the suggestion is that you seek a similar job title but with different responsibilities.

SUMMARIZING THE CHAPTER

This chapter presented another important tip for you if you want to succeed not only as an assistant principal now, but also as an educational leader in the long run. Contrary to the practice often followed by many of your colleague assistant principals around the nation, you cannot afford to become typecast in a very narrow range of professional responsibilities. You must therefore constantly seek opportunities to expand your insights and expertise. The only way to do this is to find ways to do even more than you are required to do officially.

As stated many times in this book, the assistant principalship can be much more valuable to you than simply as a job for the present. It can also be an extremely rich place for you to fine-tune and develop additional skills that you will need later in your career. In short, do your job, but if you want to succeed, do even more than your job.

10

Stay Alive Professionally

Jane Fogarty had just finished her third year as an elementary school assistant principal. Based on her self-assessment, the annual evaluation reports she had received from her principal, and also on the associate superintendent for administrative services, she had been doing a very good job as a school administrator in the district. Therefore, it was strange that Jane was now beginning to feel a bit uneasy, as if she needed to do something more in order to retain her job.

The first year as an assistant principal seemed to fly by very quickly. She was so busy all of the time, getting to understand a lot of the regular procedures that were associated with her job. She had nine years of experience as a classroom teacher, but little of that work had really seemed to get her ready for what she faced as soon as she entered the school identified as a "school administrator." That first year was really tough. First, she encountered the same reaction from staff that seems to be a regular part of the life of beginning school administrators. For example, teachers in the school who had known her as a teacher in the past seemed to shy away from opportunities to talk with her informally. The only time that people came to her was "on business." She missed the familiar chat sessions in the teachers' lounge and the opportunity to vent her frustrations with other teachers. She knew that she was an administrator now, and she could no longer open up in the same ways she did in the past.

Another part of her world that had changed drastically in the past several months was her personal life. In the past, she was able to balance her professional duties with her life as a single mother of a nine-year-old pretty well, mainly because she knew what her schedule was going to be most of the time. Her daughter was in elementary school all day, and then she always went to stay at the next-door neighbor's house until Jane came home at about 4:30. Even when Jane had to stay late for parents' nights and so forth, it was possible to set up child care arrangements because she knew well in advance when she had evening duties. Life as an assistant principal was clearly changing her ideas about the predictability of life as an educator. She now often had to meet with parents in the evening, or situations at school might arise late in the afternoon and prevent her from knowing when she would be able to get home. Thank goodness, her neighbor was understanding, but increasingly Jane was feeling guilty about her inability to provide a predictable life for her daughter.

The daily life of being an assistant was also getting Jane down. From the time she walked into her office, usually at about 7:30, to the time she left (at different hours) at night, her life seemed to consist of nothing more than phone calls; drop-in visits from teachers; "situation management" in the halls, playground, or cafeteria; and what seemed to be a thousand other things. She rarely had time to eat lunch. Every time she picked up her phone to return a call, she discovered two or three more voice mail messages left since she'd last hung up. She'd known that she would be busy, but this was beyond her imagining.

Finally, Jane was getting frustrated about her inability to engage in any reading on her own. All during her career as a classroom teacher, she had looked forward to being able to keep up with trends in teaching reading, working with special needs children, and other issues that were part of her world. When she enrolled in graduate school to pursue her master's degree and principal certification, she enjoyed reading her textbooks to learn more about her future responsibilities as a school principal. She knew that time spent as an assistant principal was probably her first step as an administrator, and she really wanted to become a principal at some point in the future.

The time, the inability to control her personal life, the difficulty of retaining her professional commitment—all of these issues were frustrating the young assistant principal. Maybe she had made a serious mistake by leaving the comfortable and predictable world of teaching.

If you are now an assistant principal, you will no doubt find Jane's discoveries in this opening scenario amusing. Like her, you are extremely busy in your job. You have to change much of your regular personal and professional routines. The notion of attending to your own learning needs seems like a luxury that is truly beyond your reach. Simply handling all of the duties of your job is quite a task. Yet if your goal is to be a principal in the foreseeable future, you may need to do your job, but continue to work. In other words, you have to do even more! For example, you cannot neglect the need to stay tuned to professional issues, recent research, and other developments in the field of education and educational research. To state the obvious, pursuing a personal professional development agenda is not always consistent with the time demands of serving as a school administrator, particularly as an assistant principal, who is so often at the mercy of "all other duties assigned."

This chapter contains information that will assist you in your pursuit of professional advancement by suggesting two broad strategies that may help in promoting personal development and refining your leadership skills. One is reading and the other is participation in professional seminars, meetings, conferences, and activities sponsored by state and national professional associations.

READ, READ, READ

Engaging in a reading agenda is a relatively simple activity to prescribe but often a difficult assignment to carry out. After all, going home to read a book or journal article after a hard day at a school in which you serve as an assistant principal is not necessarily something that you might put high on your personal "to do" list. Yet if you are going to keep current in professional practice trends, the single best way to do so is to keep up with recent literature, in the form of either journal articles or selected books. You cannot possibly become an expert on everything presented in the educational literature, but you can deliberately carve out an area in which you do most of your reading. What might be an area (or areas) in which you might wish to focus your professional reading? _____

_____

_____

_____

_____

An example of this type of "selective reading" is evident in cases where school administrators might read almost exclusively the works of William Glasser and his vision of the "Quality School." Others follow the writing and research of Carl Glickman, particularly his work on "Developmental Supervision." Neither of these authors will ever write about every single topic that needs to be addressed by effective assistant principals or other school administrators. But Glasser, Glickman, and other serious educational writers offer broad visions of effective schooling that are worthy of review, reflection, and perhaps even adoption. The key here is to recognize that no single author or series of works should be embraced as the perfect answer to all problems and issues in schools. You are, however, encouraged to keep your mind alive and well so that it can be used as a valuable repository of knowledge for improving both present and future administrative practice.

In the space below, indicate any recent books or other material you have read (or plan to read in the near future). Indicate what appeals to you about these books in relation to your work as an assistant principal. _____

_____

_____

_____

_____

PARTICIPATE IN YOUR PROFESSIONAL WORLD

The second practice recommended to help assistant principals remain alive professionally involves participation in seminars, conferences, and other activities sponsored by professional associations of principals. To a large extent, your ability to follow through with this suggestion depends on available personal or district resources. If you wish to participate in conferences and seminars, particularly those that might be offered in out-of-town locations, you are also dependent in large measure on the goodwill and permission of your principal. Simply stated, all of these suggested approaches to personal professional development cost money and time away from your job. On the other hand, even it means spending your own finances and using vacation periods, personal days, or weekends to attend professional meetings, think about doing so for at least two reasons.

First, participating in professional seminars, conferences, and other meetings is a way to learn quite a bit. These are the settings in which you can acquire at least a beginning understanding of topics that may be important to your work both now and in the future. The latest developments in curriculum, school finance, special education, bilingual education, and other important educational issues serve as the basis for many workshops, clinics, and seminars. Remember that even though you may have learned a lot in your law course in graduate school, laws and court decisions change the nature of proper administrative behavior almost daily in this country. Staying current through these types of activities is critical for both your current success and long-term development.

The second recommendation is to attend meetings and conferences not only for the opportunity to hear the latest content. By going to state and national meetings of the National Association of Elementary School Principals (NAESP), the National Association of Secondary School Principals (NASSP), the Association for Supervision and Curriculum Development (ASCD), or the state affiliates of any of these organizations, you gain a lot more than simply the information serving as content in presentations. Attending meetings of this sort will put you in contact with many other people who will, in turn, get to know you and your abilities. That form of self-marketing through personal networks will have considerable value when you begin looking around for a principalship some day. Meeting and networking with other school administrators is above all a way to help you find some of the colleagueship needed to ensure that you are not only an effective administrator, but also a person who is happy with your job.

Indicate any professional associations for school leaders in which you are currently a member, and indicate the value that you have derived from those memberships. _____

_____

_____

_____

_____

List any additional associations that you would like to join in the next year or two, and also indicate the benefits that you hope you might realize as a result of your membership. _____

_____

_____

_____

_____

Now, list any professional conferences, meetings, seminars, or clinics in which you have recently participated and indicate some of the benefits that you believe you have gained through your involvement. _____

_____

_____

_____

_____

What additional professional events would you like to attend during the next year or two? Why? _____

_____

_____

_____

_____

In addition to these suggestions regarding ways in which you can remain positive about your work as an assistant, listed below are further strategies that you may wish to consider.

Strategy 1: Find a Mentor

The single most powerful thing an assistant principal (or principal) can do to enhance personal survival and effectiveness is to find at least one experienced educational leader who can be available to share expertise related to doing your job more effectively. A mentor can also help significantly with the complex task of becoming effectively socialized into the world of school administration in general, your current role as an assistant principal, and the principalship in the future. Above all, a good mentor (or as some are now referring to this role, "critical friend") can be a person with whom you can discuss matters relating to your sense of values, ethical concerns, and many other issues that do not necessarily have a "right answer."

Do you currently have at least one mentor who is helping you while you are an assistant principal? Many people would immediately indicate that their mentor is the principal with whom they now work. For some, however, the principal does not function as a mentor, but rather as a "boss," evaluator, or in some other capacity that makes it difficult for an assistant to open up about some major concerns. If you do have a mentor now, what are some of the characteristics you have found in that person (those persons) that are particularly valuable to you? _____

_____

_____

_____

_____

What are some of the specific concerns associated with your work as an assistant principal that you believe might be addressed in a mentoring relationship? _____

_____

_____

_____

_____

Strategy 2: Develop Networks

Another strategy involves developing networks with other assistant principals. This can take several forms. For example, you may wish to make contact with the other assistants in your district or in neighboring districts to develop a "mutual support" group. You may wish to agree to get together once a month for a social gathering during which you can share some war stories about your work as an assistant. You may be surprised to learn that much of what you have been doing is shared by others. One word of caution, however: A network is not simply a "bunch of people who get together once in a while." There needs to be some common focus and agreed-upon commitment expressed to the group. If these features are not addressed, you may find that your "network" is a very temporary grouping of people, similar to the groups that "all go out together after work on Fridays." A true network can be a much more powerful grouping that helps you in your personal and professional life.

Do you know any other assistant principals in your immediate area with whom you might be able to form a mutual support network? _____

_____

_____

_____

_____

Networks have also been formed among women assistant principals. Only a few years ago this was a rarity. Now women administrator leagues and networks have appeared all over the country, generally based on the assumption that because school administration has been a man's game in the past, it is critical to develop mutually supportive arrangements among those who also want a share of the game. The same logic has been used in the establishment of networks for representatives of ethnic and racial minority groups serving as assistant principals or other school leaders.

Do you currently have any networks established with other assistant principals? _____

_____

_____

_____

_____

In what specific ways might your network assist you in dealing with concerns and issues you face each day as an assistant principal? _____

_____

_____

_____

_____

Strategy 3: Maintain Personal and Family Support

One additional form of support may be the most obvious one, but it can be overlooked. Often, the most powerful way to help people is found in one's natural, immediate environment. As you carry out your duties as an assistant principal, it is likely that your world will be filled with so many new responsibilities, people, and activities that the many competing demands and interests will become overwhelming. Suddenly, things and events that were important to you only a few months ago seem distant and less important as you work hard to develop a professional identity and self-image. Although that may be understandable, it is critical to keep a personal focus on what is truly important in your life. Demands of a professional nature are important; the roots and foundation in your personal and family life are even more important and will be with you well beyond your career as the assistant principal of a school.

The first recommendation, then, is to make certain that, whenever possible, you do whatever is needed and reasonable to maintain some sense of normality in your personal life. Do not ignore family and friends. Keep your compass and perspective; don't forget what is really important to you. Remember that you can be a very effective and successful leader even if you take a night off just to sit with your family in front of the television to watch a sitcom.

The second recommendation is related to your need to maintain your health. Critically ill assistant principals are not terribly effective. Do not neglect matters of personal health, fitness, and well-being. This is important not only in matters of physical well-being, but also emotional, intellectual, and even spiritual health. Go to the doctor when you are sick and for regular examinations, eat right, and don't fall into the administrator-as-martyr syndrome that seemingly rewards people for skipping breakfast, never eating lunch, and drinking coffee all day. Take care of yourself. Get out of your office and forget about work once in a while.

With regard to intellectual well-being, do something that challenges your mental capacity. Some assistants take university courses or participate in study groups that have nothing to do with the field of education as a way to keep their minds sharp. Engage in activities that may seem to have nothing to do with schools but serve as a way to maintain your spiritual core.

It is not possible to prescribe all of the things that you might do to ensure that you maintain a balance in your priorities as an assistant principal of a school. Happiness at home is, of course, not a guarantee of effective performance in your work life, and trouble in your personal life does not always mean failure at school. The message here is that it is not only a good idea for assistant principals to place their own needs above other issues, but in many ways a critical responsibility.

List some of the ways you intend to spend more time with your family, engage in leisure activities, or simply take care of yourself during the next several months. _____

_____

_____

_____

_____

What are some of the personal and professional benefits that you hope to achieve? _____

_____

_____

_____

_____

SUMMARIZING THE CHAPTER

This chapter addressed the importance of an effective school leader, whether an assistant principal or a principal, attending to personal and professional well-being. You are involved in a complex, challenging, and often stressful career. You are expected to meet the demands of many different and often competing audiences each day. Your principal will expect you to carry out assigned tasks effectively. Teachers want you to intervene on their behalf in many different matters. Students look to you in many different ways. Parents expect you to provide answers—particularly answers that they will like. Your family continues to expect you to behave the same way you did when you were a teacher. The list of competing expectations could fill many pages in this book.

In the long run, the only effective way for you to meet the many challenges of your job is to remain tuned in to your inner sense of duty and professional responsibility. Numerous suggestions were offered here as ways to help you accomplish just that and enjoy your role more.

11

Stay Positive

Roberta Clayton was finishing her first year as the assistant principal of Forest View Elementary School, a relatively new school on the east side of Junction City. She had spent nine years as a classroom teacher in the district, and had spent nearly an entire year sending out applications for an administrative position in Junction City as well as several other local school systems. She thought about the move from the classroom to an administrative office for a long time before enrolling in a principalship program at a local university. She loved to teach, but the thought of being able to have a positive impact on all the students in a school made her decide to move to a different career path as an educator. She knew that her first step would probably be into an assistant principalship, but she was eager to begin a new chapter in her work life.

Soon after applying, she was invited to serve as the assistant principal at Forest View. She was delighted to receive the offer. She knew several of the teachers at Forest View, and she had heard many great things about the school, its principal, staff, and the surrounding community. She was very enthusiastic about the opportunity to work with and learn from Robb Krause, the principal. He had a reputation as a no-nonsense administrator and a terrific mentor to many young administrators who now worked across the district. She eagerly agreed to take the job, almost before the superintendent had completed asking her if she was still interested.

Robb quickly turned out to be the kind of principal that she had hoped for, one who would assist her in this "new world" of school leadership. He made it clear that he had high expectations for Roberta, and that he would always be available to help her when she needed him. He was, however, also a firm believer that the best way to learn about the principalship was "to step right in and do the job—warts and all." He told her that she would be busy and that there would probably be many times when she would be ready to hand in her keys and go back to the classroom. If she made it through the first year or so, she would be ready to start thinking about looking for a principalship pretty soon.

Robb was not kidding about putting Roberta on the firing line as soon as possible. He assigned her the duties of testing coordinator, parent-community liaison, and inservice director. In addition, she had to do all of the other traditional duties of any assistant principal—discipline, attendance, supervision in the halls and on the playground, covering the building in his absence, and handling all emergencies that popped up during the course of a day. He knew that it would not be in Roberta's best interests to assign her to do nothing but student discipline in the school, so he indicated that he would be sharing that responsibility with her. Nevertheless, meeting with students who had misbehaved was a big part of her job as an assistant. Robb knew that she had to master this responsibility if she was ever to be seen as a viable candidate for most principalships.

Every day seemed to be filled with an endless list of challenges. In addition to stacks of discipline referrals and follow-up conferences with students, Roberta seemed always to have lines of parents waiting to see her about one matter or another. Working with custodians and other classified staff members was both a pleasure (because it allowed her to get away from her office) and a frequent source of frustration. She really knew very little about the management of the school building, and some of the union contract provisions seemed to contradict her natural inclination to make certain decisions. Most of her graduate courses in school administration focused on theory, curriculum, instruction, and other aspects of what she thought were the really important aspects of working in a school. She was increasingly frustrated by feeling very much like a whirling top that had to respond to everyone, but realizing, too, that she had a job to do each day.

In early March, Roberta began to think very seriously about exploring a different alternative to her new role as a school administrator. She was contemplating contacting the Office of Human Resources about the possibility of returning to her more comfortable and familiar role as a classroom teacher again next year. She was increasingly beginning to think that she was never going to be able to relax and enjoy being in the administrative office. She missed the friendship of other teachers, the predictability of work in the classroom, and above all, she missed her students. She decided that the next day she would go to Robb and admit her feelings of having made a horrible mistake. She felt that she simply did not have "the right stuff" to make her an effective school leader.

Some who read this opening scenario might quickly identify with Roberta's feelings as a beginning school administrator. It is not only that the job is difficult (and it is!), but that as an administrator you often feel as if you cannot get much accomplished in any regular way. Maybe it is simply not worth all of the daily headaches and heartbreaks that a person must experience in order to be an effective assistant principal.

Yet if there were not people, like you, who are willing to take on the risks and challenges associated with being an assistant principal, we would all soon begin to suffer from a serious lack of talented people ready to step into principalships. We know that effective schools require effective leadership by committed and experienced principals. If we cannot find excellent principals who care about their schools, education, and, above all, students, what will be the future of education in this country?

The purpose of this final chapter is to offer you, as an assistant principal (or prospective assistant principal), a suggestion that may actually surpass all others presented in the earlier chapters. It touches on all other recommendations. Simply, be as positive and enthusiastic as you can about yourself, your job, your colleagues, your students, your community, and your school district. Admittedly, this is not always an easy thing to do. A big part of your life as an administrator automatically involves problem solving and being "knee-deep in alligators." It is more than a little tempting to spend a lot (most?) of your time feeling bad about your job as an assistant principal. Remember the example of Roberta in the opening pages? Despite the efforts of her principal to give her a wide variety of experiences, she spent the majority of her time dealing with conflict. She had to deal with disciplinary problems and see a lot of students in trouble. As a result, she no doubt met with many unhappy parents, too.

Because you work as an assistant principal, your boss assigns you many jobs that have to be described as somewhat less than glamorous. As a school administrator, however, you are also an insider in terms of getting to know what is really going on in your district and school. Therefore, you are often able to learn about some of the more serious problems in your organization. The word *assistant* in your title means that you often have little direct control over the problems you have to deal with. Even if you could fix things, you might not be able to do so because of your role. You really have to guard against becoming cynical by investing too much time in dwelling on the worst features of your life as an educator.

What are some of the current problems facing your school or district that frustrate you the most? _____

_____

_____

_____

_____

POSITIVE ATTITUDE IS A CAREER BUILDER

Stop to think about what dwelling on the many problems you face might do for you as you begin to build your career as an educational leader. Imagine that you are involved in searching for the new principal of your school. Also, think about the reaction you would have to applicants for the position if they came to the job interview and spent a good deal of time criticizing or complaining about their present school, administrators, teachers, or school district. Compare the impressions that you might have of such people with candidates who came forward with a reputation for being positive, enthusiastic, and boosters of their present situation. Given those two alternatives as applicants, if equally qualified for the principalship, most (if not all) school systems will quickly select the person who is positive. After all, there is something quite attractive about cheerleaders, especially if you envision them leading the cheers for where you now work.

Building the image of someone who is enthusiastic and happy cannot be accomplished in only the few weeks during which you might be an active candidate for a job, of course. A reputation as a team player who can make positive contributions as a future principal gets built over a rather long period of time and as the result of many things. It must also be seen as a consistent approach to your job. After all, people who seem to be "up" one day and very negative the next day are quickly characterized as unpredictable and not necessarily leadership material. One of the things it is very important to remember is that you will be on stage during your entire career. Whether you know it or not (and even if you do not want this to be the case), people tend to view current assistant principals as potential candidates for many different future administrative positions. As soon as it becomes clear that a principal is retiring, being transferred, or leaving for any reason, people tend to think of possible candidates for replacement. If your goal is to move to another position after the assistant principalship, you want to be on that list of reasonable choices. The way to do that is to be visible and be perceived as a team player who would be a positive addition to a school. Even if you wish to remain as an assistant, it is important that you be known as someone who would be an asset to any school.

What are some of the ways in which you believe that you currently display a positive attitude to your school and work as an assistant principal?

_____

_____

_____

_____

Be extremely sensitive to the image that you project to others. When you are at meetings with people from other schools, it is critical that you be a cheerleader for your present students, teachers, principal, school, and district. No matter what others may say or believe about your current situation, it is critical that your public stance be one of support and commitment to the best place you can possibly be—at least for now. Taking any other stance creates an image that you do not want. You do not want anyone to fear what you might do or say about their school if you became their principal. If you were to be chosen as the leader of "our school," people would want to believe that you would support them as much as you support others in your present position.

Regardless of any problems that might exist in your present school or district, list ten or more features in your present situation that make it a good place in which to work. _____

_____

_____

_____

_____

_____

_____

_____

_____

_____

Make a copy of the above list and read it over each time you head out of your office door. Remember the best features of your work environment. Do not develop a similar listing of problems and shortcomings. Frankly, even if saying these things would not have a negative effect on your career, no one really wants to hear your gripes or problems you are having back home. It is similar to sitting on a three-hour airplane flight, being forced to listen to an unhappy flight attendant share war stories about the pay cut taken by the union in order to keep the airline financially solvent. It may make the flight attendant feel good to share the story, but in the long run, who cares? What's more, does it ensure that your flight is safe or on time?

Above all, stay positive, be enthusiastic, and always project an image that allows people to have confidence that you will be the same kind of person in your next job. Remember, when you have a job as an administrator you become extremely visible to everyone who works in the school. As a result, your ability to model a positive attitude is a very important skill that helps others cope with personal frustrations as workers: If the boss can take it, so can I!

FINAL OBSERVATIONS

Throughout the chapters of this book, a number of strategies have been suggested to assist you in having a successful experience as an assistant principal. As noted earlier, your job is not only very demanding, but is often filled with many frustrations. In this closing section you are invited to reflect on what you have read and to consider your own circumstances as an educational leader.

If you are currently an assistant principal who wishes to become a principal in the near future, review the suggested learning strategies presented in the previous chapters of this book. Identify those issues that you believe are most relevant to you, and indicate what you plan to do during the next year or two. For example, you might wish to identify a few books that you would like to read as a way to stay alive professionally. Alternatively, what are the professional associations that you believe you need to join? _____

_____

_____

_____

_____

If you are not currently an administrator, but you are planning to begin your administrative career as an assistant principal, you may wish to identify which of the strategies listed in this book will help you in planning ways to ensure your service as an assistant principal can be a powerful beginning to your personal formation as an educational leader.

_____

_____

_____

_____

As educating our nation's children becomes an ever-increasingly complex task, it is clear that strong leadership is needed to ensure that schools are as effective as possible in reaching out to help their students. You may personally see the job of assistant principal as the position from which you some day hope to retire. Or, you may believe that the assistant principalship is a transitional experience that is needed in your career to prepare you for other future jobs. While you are in the role now (or will be in the near future), remember that despite any frustrations that may come your way, you are doing an incredibly important job. Schools are challenging organizations, and they require the "best and brightest" leaders to direct the efforts of all who work in them. Never lose that focus, and the job will continue to be something that you enjoy doing. Everyone wins in that case.

Index

**CORWIN
PRESS**

The Corwin Press logo—a raven striding across an open book—represents the union of courage and learning. Corwin Press is committed to improving education for all learners by publishing books and other professional development resources for those serving the field of K–12 education. By providing practical, hands-on materials, Corwin Press continues to carry out the promise of its motto: **"Helping Educators Do Their Work Better."**